Rebbe Nachman of Breslov

The Rebbe's Pharmacy

Chizuk and Inspiration for Today's Spiritual Illnesses

By Lev Moshe Leventer

Inspired by the teachings of
Rabbi Nissan Dovid Kivak, Shlita

Published by
Meirat Eynaim Institute
1 Menachem Meshiv Street,
Jerusalem, Israel

November, 2020

Copyright by Lev Moshe Leventer ©
All rights reserved

For questions and comments,
or to order copies of the book
you may contact:

In Israel
Phone: 02-664-5547
Fax: 0773182144
Email: office@meirat.org

In the U.S.
321 Route 59, Suite W6
Tallman, NY 10982
Phone: 917-657- 0680
Email: usaoffice@meirat.org

In England
108 Geldeston Road,
London E5 8RS
Email: ukoffice@meirat.org

BS"D

The Rebbe's Pharmacy

Chizuk and Inspiration for Today's Spiritual Illnesses

The Rebbe's Pharmacy

Chizuk and Inspiration for Today's Spiritual Illnesses

Edited by R' Avrohom Hersh Singer and Mrs Shifra Ebbing

Graphics by Studio TCH

Printed by Defus Ateret
Jerusalem, Israel

Other books by the same author:
*Hashem Is Your Friend:
A Guide to Hisbodedus*

לע"נ
הרב נפתלי
הירץ בן צבי
ממשפחת שטיינברג

Dedicated in Loving Memory of Nethaniel Steinberg

Dedicated in honor of the newly-weds Shimon ben Sarah Itah and Simchah bas Ilana.

May they be blessed to build a beis ne'eman beYisroel, a bounty of shefa from the Abishter, and joyous shalom bayis ad 120!

לע"נ האשה החשובה

מרת פריידא רחל בת ר' יחזקאל יוסף ע"ה

A selfless woman of valor who tirelessly dedicated her life to healing the bodies and souls of the Jewish nation.

ת.נ.צ.ב.ה.

Dedicated in Loving Memory of Our Parents:

Max And Jenny Weil

משה מנחם בן החבר חיים אליהו ומרים וייל

חיה גיטל בת הרב מרדכי ושרה

Rabbi William and Miriam Eidelsberg

הרב זאב בן דוד וחיה

מרים רש"י בת משה חיים הכהן וחוה

From Dr. Daniel and Dee-Da Weil

With gratitude to Hashem for the blessing of my wife, Esther bas Daniel HaLevi, an Eshes Chayil, and our wonderful children and grandchildren.

Dedicated in honor of Rifka Miriam bas Tzviah Binah for a refuah shleimah.

לעילוי נשמת
נפתלי
מתתיהו בן ר'
דוד יוסף

Dedicated in Loving Memory of

Dr. Ira and Diana Leventer,

of Blessed Memory

and

Edward and Wanda Anzicek,

of Blessed Memory

Dedicated in Loving Memory of Binyamin ben Chaim, of Blessed Memory

Dedicated in honor of Dr. Yehuda Frischman, for all he does to bring Torah and especially Rebbe Nachman's teachings to the world through his work as a real doctor of Traditional Jewish Medicine. May he continue to be blessed to help others to connect to the One Above, and may we continue to skip through life together ad meah v'esrim shanah.

Table of Contents

Author's Note   *1*

Introduction   *5*

Chizuk in Avodas Hashem

Chapter One: *14*

The Illness: I feel glued to my bed and I can't get up in the morning.

The Rebbe's Prescription: The whole entire world was created just for you to serve Hashem! (Based on Likutei Mohoran I, 17)

Chapter Two: *24*

The Illness: Sometimes, I have good days and I can do avodas Hashem. But other days, I have no inspiration and I don't do anything.

The Rebbe's Prescription: When you realize that the main thing is your desire to serve Hashem; there are no more bad days. (Based on Likutei Mohoran I, 33, and Sichos HaRan, 14)

Chapter Three: *33*

The Illness: It seems like there is an alien in my mind who is sending my thoughts on a rollercoaster out of my control.

The Rebbe's Prescription: Don't stop to think! Just keep doing avodas Hashem, and eventually the alien will go away. (Based on Likutei Mohoran I, 72)

Chapter Four: 41

The Illness: Day after day passes me by and I'm not able to accomplish anything in my learning.

The Rebbe's Prescription: By focusing on one day at a time and learning small daily portions, you will see incredible progress. (Based on Likutei Mohoran I, 27)

Chapter Five: 56

The Illness: No matter how many layers I put on, my avodas Hashem still feels freezing cold.

The Rebbe's Prescription: By living with the awareness that Hashem is mamash with you, you can find a spark in your avodah. (Based on Likutei Mohoran I, 62:2)

Chizuk in Emunah

Chapter Six: 64

The Illness: My heart is so twisted with questions and doubts about Hashem and His ways.

The Rebbe's Prescription: Deep inside your heart there is a computer chip of faith that can help you fly over all of your questions and doubts. (Based on Likutei Mohoran I, 64)

Chapter Seven: 77

The Illness: It feels like I have to work very hard to do mitzvos, and I'm always falling short.

The Rebbe's Prescription: By strengthening your faith in yourself, serving Hashem becomes easy and enjoyable. (Based on Likutei Mohoran II, 86 and Likutei Halachos, Pikadon 5:7)

Chapter Eight: 85

The Illness: It seems like everything in my life is going wrong and I never get a break.

The Rebbe's Prescription: Even the midst of the worst suffering, you can find moments of relief and glimmers of hope that will carry you to salvation. (Based on Likutei Mohoran I, 185)

Chizuk in Simchah

Chapter Nine: 96

The Illness: I feel so depressed and lazy, and I have no strength for avodas Hashem.

The Rebbe's Prescription: The light from one mitzvah can push away all the sadness and inspire you to serve Hashem with joy! (Based on Likutei Mohoran, 282)

Chapter Ten: 108

The Illness: No matter what I do, I can't find a way to be happy.

The Rebbe's Prescription: Sometimes, you simply need to "fake it till you make it," and just do something silly. (Based on Likutei Halachos, Nefilas Apayim 4)

Chizuk in Teshuvah

Chapter Eleven: 120

The Illness: Whenever I try to do teshuvah, I usually end up falling further away from Hashem.

The Rebbe's Prescription: At the same time that you must try to reach higher, you must also strengthen yourself and hold yourself up. (Based on Likutei Mohoran I, 6)

Chapter Twelve: 132

The Illness: I know Hashem exists, but I can't find Him in my life. I've fallen so far and I'm completely lost.

The Rebbe's Prescription: Even in the darkest and most contaminated places Hashem can be found: You just have to search for Him. (Based on Likutei Mohoran II, 12)

Chapter Thirteen: 140

The Illness: I've fallen so deep into physical desire that I can't feel the kedushah of my neshamah.

The Rebbe's Prescription: By comparing yourself to a goy, you can see that your soul is shining with a brilliant holiness. (Based on Likutei Halachos, Reishis Hagez 4)

Chapter Fourteen: 147

The Illness: I am who I am, and there's no way I'll ever be able to change.

The Rebbe's Prescription: You must believe that you have the ability to hit the "erase" button and completely start over at any moment! (Based on Likutei Halachos, Krias HaTorah 6)

Chapter Fifteen: 159

The Illness: I've made such incredible mistakes that I feel like my avodas Hashem is worthless.

The Rebbe's Prescription: The further you fall away from Hashem, the more important your mitzvos are. (Based on Likutei Halachos, Birkas Hareyach 3)

Chizuk in Connecting to Tzaddikim

Chapter Sixteen: 170

The Illness: I would like to purify myself and serve Hashem like a tzaddik; but every time I try, it feels like Hashem is pushing me further away.

The Rebbe's Prescription: The main difference between a tzaddik and an average Jew is that a tzaddik never gives up. (Based on Likutei Mohoran II, 48)

Chapter Seventeen: 179

The Illness: I feel like I'm all alone in my suffering, and there's no one who knows how to help me.

The Rebbe's Prescription: In each generation there is a great tzaddik who can diagnose and heal all illnesses. Search for him! (Based on Likutei Mohoran I, 30)

Author's Note

In order to understand the purpose of this book, I will first give a brief background of the teachings of Breslov.

Rebbe Nachman made the computer chip and Reb Nosson built the computer.

Rebbe Nachman *zt"l*, a great grandson of the Baal Shem Tov *zt"l*, wrote the first Breslov sefer, Likutei Mohoran, around the beginning of the nineteenth century. Likutei Mohoran could be compared to a very advanced computer chip. Even though it is relatively small, it contains an enormous amount of information. In fact, it is almost as if the entire book is one huge table of contents, in which each sentence is a new chapter heading that requires in-depth explanation (see the introduction to Likutei Mohoran written by Reb Nosson, *zt"l*). By writing in such a fashion, Rebbe Nachman was able to give over an unbelievable amount of Torah in the course of his very brief lifetime.

However, much like a computer chip, Likutei Mohoran is very difficult to grasp on its own. Without the electronic device to plug it into – in other words, the vessel which can display and expand its information – it is hard to understand each one of the "chapter headings" and how they relate to one another.

Therefore, Rebbe Nachman instructed his primary pupil, Reb Nosson, to expound upon his teachings (see Chayei Mohoran, 2). He told him to explain the ideas in his sefer and connect them to specific halachos in the Shulchan Aruch.

In fulfillment of his Rebbe's request, Reb Nosson wrote Likutei Halachos, which can be compared to the computer through which we can view the information that is on Rebbe Nachman's compact chip. From the one small sefer of Likutei Mohoran, Reb Nosson wrote eight sefarim which flesh out many of the chapter headings and clarify the Torah of Rebbe Nachman.

Additionally, by relating the teachings of Rebbe Nachman to specific halachos – many of which we fulfill on a regular basis – Reb Nosson makes it possible for us to attach ourselves to the Rebbe's Torah through our practice of mitzvos. Reb Nosson also brings the Torah of Rebbe Nachman into our lives in such a way that it is possible for us to relate to it on a personal level. Thus, it is only through the teachings of Reb Nosson that we can truly access the exalted inspiration and wisdom of Likutei Mohoran.

In our generation we fail to receive the true strength and inspiration of Breslov teachings.

However, due to the severe decline in spiritual capacity and the poor clarity of mind of our generation, many of us find it hard to grasp the teachings of Reb Nosson themselves, and even Likutei Halachos seems beyond our reach.

We've fallen so far that not only is there is a gap between us and Rebbe Nachman, there is also a gap between us and Reb Nosson. Thus, although we have all the spiritual wealth in the world right at our fingertips (see Likutei Mohoran I, 60), it is still unaccessible to us.

Only through the carriers of the Breslov tradition of today can we access the Torah of Rebbe Nachman.

Therefore, it is pertinent for us to connect to the true talmidim of Rebbe Nachman of our generation who can help us bridge the gap. We must find the carriers of the oral Breslov tradition who understand how to help us bring the teachings of Rebbe Nachman and Reb Nosson into our avodas Hashem and daily trials and tribulations (see Likutei Halachos, Sheluchim 5).

In the process of searching for such guidance, I've found the teachings of Reb Nissan Dovid Kivak, *shlit"a*, to be incredibly useful. Through his unfathomably deep understand of Breslov Torah and profound insight into the struggles of our generation, Reb Nissan Dovid is able to show Jews from all backgrounds and cultures how to relate to the wondrous advice of Rebbe Nachman and incorporate it into their lives.

It is his influence which inspired me to begin writing, and his guidance in the teachings of Breslov which has helped me to be able to explain the Torah of Rebbe Nachman to our generation.

"The Rebbe's Pharmacy" is meant to bring the light of Rebbe Nachman down into the darkness of today's world.

This is the purpose of this book: to make the amazingly practical and inspirational advice of Breslov chassidus more accessible, and to bring the brilliant spiritual light of Rebbe Nachman – which has the ability to save us from all of our suffering and elevate us closer to Hashem – into the depths of spiritual despair of today's modern world.

It is not a book of *chidushim* based on Breslov teachings. Rather, it is a vessel for the Torah of Rebbe Nachman which is intended to help our generation find new strength in avodas Hashem, emunah, simchah, teshuvah, and connection to tzaddikim.

This book is not just for Breslover chassidim, rather it is for anyone who's searching for Hashem.

One more introductory point that I will make is that one does not need to identify himself as a *Breslover chasid* in order to get *chizuk* from this book. Rather, it is for all those who have not given up on doing teshuva and coming closer to Hashem. It is for all those who still have hope of overcoming their bad midos and desires. It is for all those who long to attach themselves constantly to avodas Hashem with love and awe. It is meant to guide any Jew who is searching for Hashem to find the help that he needs to face the challenges of this generation.

Nevertheless, the content of this book is directed primarily to orthodox Jews. Therefore, there are many examples of everyday religious life that a secular person would not understand. Additionally, there are many colloquial words from Hebrew and Yiddish which are used exclusively in the orthodox vernacular. Since this is the target audience for the book, I did not feel it was necessary to make a glossary of the non-English words. However, a secular Jew or non-Jew should not be discouraged from reading this book, since the general ideas are accessible to all, even without understanding certain words or examples here and there.

To conclude with words of blessing, may we all merit to follow in the path of the tzadikim and find true spiritual healing for all of our illnesses, amen!

Sincerely,
Lev Moshe Leventer
The Author

Elul, 5780
Jerusalem, Israel

Introduction

Whatever is wrong, today there is a pill to fix it.

Nowadays, there's a pill for everything. There's a pill for headaches and a pill for coughs. There's a pill for allergies and a pill for nausea. There's a pill for fevers and another pill for sore throats. There's a pill for back pain, neck pain, muscle pain, stomach pain, chest pain, joint pain, and tooth pain. Whatever slight discomfort we have in our body, there's a pill to take care of it.

In addition, there are countless pills for strengthening our health. There's a pill for vitamins A, B, C, D, etc. There's a pill for all the types of vitamin B, and there's even a pill with all the vitamins put together.

If we have hair-loss, there's a pill for that. If we want to build muscle mass and get really strong, there's a pill for that. If we want to quit smoking, there's a pill for that. If we have bad acne, there's a pill for that. If we want to lose weight, there are a ton of pills for that.

If we feel tired, there is a pill to wake us up. If we can't sleep at night, there's a pill to knock us out. If we feel down and depressed, there's a pill to make us feel like everything is just yummy and fine. If we feel nervous and anxious, there's a pill to calm us down and make everything nice and mellow. If we find ourselves struggling in school and at work because we simply can't sit down and focus, there's even a pill that can help us to concentrate our mind and be successful.

Going to the pharmacy is like going to the grocery store. Even better, it's like going to Walmart. Everything you could possibly need in life, you can find it in a pill.

We are even willing to deal with the numerous side-effects of the pills, since there is another pill which takes care of the side-effects. For example, when we feel a little depressed, we take a pill which numbs our bitterness. The problem is that it makes us nauseous, so we have to take another pill for nausea. However, that pill makes us very tired, so we have to take another pill to shake off our drowsiness. Thus, we go from one to the next; until we find ourselves taking a cocktail of pills, just because we felt lonely.

Some of these pills are so enjoyable, that we take them even if we don't have the required symptoms. After a little while, we become addicted to them and we can't remember what life was like beforehand. The pills become a part of who we are and how we experience this world. The desire and attachment to a lot of these feel-good pills is so great, that there's a massive black-market which makes them available to those without prescriptions.

These pills are not dealing with our core spiritual issues.

When we take a step back and look at this picture, there are some big questions which arise: What are we missing so badly in our lives, which cause us to take so many pills? Up until a hundred years ago, almost none of these pills existed. Was life really so awful? Is it so much better now? Most of us would agree, that even with all of our incessant pill-popping, we are much less happier and satisfied with our lives than in previous generations. So why do we do it?

The answer is that we are going through physical, emotional, and/or psychological pain which we just can't deal with. This pain and suffering is not new. Fevers, flus, sinus infections, and stomach problems are not unique to our generation. Likewise, depression and anxiety have been around since the beginning of mankind, as well as hair-loss and weight-gain. What's changed is our ability to cope; we just can't deal with these things anymore.

Every slight physical discomfort throws us into such deep agony, that our society is willing to invest literally trillions of dollars to make pills which will take away our pain. Any slight deformity in our physical appearance makes us so socially insecure, that we're willing to take a pill and deal with the crazy side-effects. All the more so, the emotional struggles we go through make us give up completely on life, so we had better make a pill for that. Any little thing that goes wrong with our marriage, our children, or our job, drives us up the wall. Until, finally, we find that pill which makes us feel just right.

The problem is that these pills are like putting small Band-Aids on an internal wound. They may seem to help, but only for a little while. They relieve us of our pain temporarily, but soon enough, it comes right back, often even stronger than before. This is because these pills don't deal with the root of our sickness.

They're not able to heal the source of the problem: our deep, spiritual brokenness. We feel completely lost and distant from Hashem. We live our life without really thinking about Him. We attribute our wealth to our own efforts and our debt to our bad mazal. We are constantly angry and frustrated when things don't go our way, and we have little to no real faith in Hashem that everything is for the best. We feel so physically and spiritually weak that we can barely get out of bed in the morning and go to shul.

We follow halachah like it's an instruction booklet and we are mechanical robots. For some of us, the machinery has totally broken down and we stop going through the motions altogether, G-d forbid.

We've given up on finding any inspiration in *avodas Hashem*. Davening feels like pulling teeth, so we spend most of it in the coffee room. If we have any enjoyment from learning, it's probably from the *kavod* we get from others. Sometimes, we can't wait until Shabbos is over, and we can do what we really want. The same is true with the other mitzvos as well.

We're going through the motions and playing the *frum* game, but deep down inside, there is a huge void. So we try to fill it with all the physical desires of this world. However, even after a big, juicy twelve oz. steak, we still feel like we're missing something. Even the fanciest suit, fastest sports-car, and hugest mansion leave us feeling unsatisfied at the end of the day. All the pills in the world are not enough to truly heal our spiritual pain.

There is hope: There is another pharmacy which has the cure for our body and soul.

In the midst of all of this darkness, however, there is another pharmacy. It is very hidden – tucked away inside some old books – so most of us don't even notice it. To those of us who walk by and see it, it seems so ancient and outdated that we think it couldn't possibly have the pills which would be able to heal our modern-day illnesses. Compared to the fancy, new pharmacy, with all of its flashing lights and glamorous pictures, this old-fashioned pharmacy doesn't look so promising. So we just keep on walking and continue searching for our happiness in the new pharmacy, trying this pill and that, with the false hope that maybe the new pill might be the answer to all our problems.

However, even though on the outside the old pharmacy may not look like much, on the inside it has all of the medicine we need to cure our illnesses. It has pills for physical pain, and emotional suffering, as well as psychological distress. They can give us incredible strength when we're weak, as well as take away all of our anxiety and worries- and make us feel truly happy and satisfied with our life. These pills can also give us hope for the future, no matter how dismal our situation may be and give us the courage to withstand the darkest and most fearsome storms. It also has pills that make us feel deeply loved and taken care of as well as grateful-and inspire our heart to sing. They can also make us feel warm in the winter, and cool us down in the summer. These pills can also make us feel good about the person we are, even with all of our deficiencies, as well as comfort us and make us feel like we're never alone.

This pharmacy has medicine which heals the source of all our suffering.

The pills from the old pharmacy don't just take away the symptoms; rather they cure us of the underlying issues and completely restore our soul. They can uproot our illness from its core and heal us forever. They can transform us from the inside, the result being that all of our symptoms automatically go away. They can quench our dried-up soul with the waters of Gan Eden. They can blow off all of the countless layers of ash which have collected on top of our *neshamah*, and reignite our spiritual flame.

Maybe, we've already looked at old pharmacies tucked away in other books similar to this one, and we didn't find a pill to suit our modern-day needs; Perhaps consider that this pharmacy is a little different. Perhaps, it *really* has what we need. Perhaps, its pills were created specifically for the pain and suffering of our generation, and not just for the days of old. Maybe, we should go in and give it a try…

This is the Rebbe's Pharmacy – the teachings of Rebbe Nachman of Breslov.

Even though Rebbe Nachman lived more than two hundred years ago, his Torah is becoming more and more relevant as time goes on. His *sefarim* and present-day *talmidim* – the carriers of the Breslov tradition – are bringing hundreds of thousands of people closer to their Creator. His teachings are helping Jews from all walks of life and levels of observance to reach higher levels in *avodas Hashem*.

To our Roshei Yeshivos, who are already deeply attached to the Torah, Rebbe Nachman shows how to achieve even greater faith in Hashem. To our *yeshivah bachurim* who are struggling to sit and learn, the Rebbe gives the strength to be able to settle their mind and find inspiration in their *avodas Hashem*. To our *avreichim* who are lost in despair from their insurmountable debts, the Rebbe gives the courage to never give up and to daven with all their heart until Hashem answers their prayers. To the worst sinners, Rebbe Nachman reveals that Hashem is still with them and shows them the way out of their darkness. To Jews who grew up with little to no Torah at all, and even to *goyim* and those with absolutely no connection, the Rebbe gives hope and inspiration and brings them into the realm of *kedushah*.

The Rebbe's pills were designed specifically for today's illnesses.

Rebbe Nachman foresaw the path that the world in general and the Jewish people in particular, were going to take until the days of Mashiach. He foresaw the darkness of atheism that was going to take over the world, as well as the unbelievable outbreak of physical desire which was going to infest modern-day society. He foresaw the bitterness of depression and other emotional illnesses that were going to infect the masses, as well as the brokenness, disconnect, and loneliness which people of our generation were going to feel.

Not only that, he even foresaw the effect that all of these things would have on *frum* Jews. He understood how even someone who would continue to follow the Torah in this day and age, would be incredibly tested in all of his physical desires, and he understood that many would fall. He understood just how weak our *emunah* would become and how empty our life would feel. He understood how lifeless our *avodas Hashem* would become, and how deep our emotional and spiritual suffering would be.

In light of his great vision and insight, Rebbe Nachman prepared countless remedies for us to heal all of our sicknesses. He wrote Torah which would be able to strengthen us, even in the most impossible situations. He gave us hope in the face of today's seemingly insurmountable challenges. His teachings talk directly to each one of us and inspire us to never give up, and to serve Hashem with all our hearts.

The world is starting to find that the Rebbe's pills can heal us and bring us closer to Hashem.

Thus, we see that the Breslov fire is spreading over the entire world. In the late eighties, there were perhaps a few hundred people coming to Uman – the gravesite of Rebbe Nachman – for Rosh Hashanah. Over the past thirty years, those few hundred have grown to estimations of between seventy to eighty thousand. It has become a pilgrimage for Jews from countless backgrounds, countries, and traditions. They are so inspired by the Rebbe's Rosh Hashanah, that they wouldn't miss it for the world.

And those who have come to Uman are only a select few who were able to overcome all of the enormous obstacles to get there, such as the ridiculous price of the tickets, the difficulties of travel, and family members or societal pressures which prevent them from going, among countless others. The actual number of people learning Rebbe Nachman's *sefarim* today and drawing true strength and inspiration is exponentially higher than the number of people who make it to Uman.

It's clear that many of us are searching for another cure. We're tired of all the new pills from the new pharmacy that don't address our core problems. We are looking for something real: a deep spiritual strength and light. And we are finding it in the teachings of Rebbe Nachman. Finally, we have found the ultimate pill to bring us back to life and create lasting happiness and contentment. We have found "the medicine," which can bring us truly closer to Hashem.

12 | The Rebbe's Pharmacy

Chizuk in Avodas Hashem

Chapter One

The Illness: I feel glued to my bed and I can't get up in the morning.

Sometimes, it can seem almost impossible to get out of bed in the morning. Maybe we ate too much the night before, or we had a few too many drinks. Perhaps, we feel so dismal and depressed with our life that we simply have no motivation to keep going. Maybe, it's the side-effects of the sleep medicine we took, or perhaps we just went to sleep way too late. Whatever the reason is, we're stuck.

We hit the snooze button once, and then twice, but no matter how many times our alarm goes off it will not get us out of bed. We lay there trying to imagine ways to escape all of our responsibilities for that day. We've already used up all of our sick-days at work, kollel, or yeshivah, but maybe we could come up with a really creative excuse. We dream of just being able to stay in bed and watch videos all day long, and if we can think of a good excuse, this dream becomes a reality and we just don't get up!

But if nothing comes to mind, we wait until the last possible minute. Then, we manage to roll out of bed, run to shul, throw on our tallis and tefillin, flip through the pages of our siddur, and speed off to work, kollel or yeshivah.

The Rebbe's Prescription: The whole entire world was created just for you to serve Hashem! (Based on Likutei Mohoran I, 17)

By not recognizing our own spiritual power, we have no motivation for *avodas Hashem*.

What we don't realize is just how important we really are. We think: "What's the big deal if I skip most of *Pesukei d'Zimra*? What does it matter if I leave shul right after *kedushah*? What does it matter if I don't daven at all?! The world will be just fine if I take a half an hour break from morning *seder* to eat breakfast. Don't I deserve a day of vacation from yeshivah?" Thus, since we devalue the importance of our *avodah*, we have no motivation to get out of bed.

The splendor and *kavod* which we give to Hashem was the inspiration for the entire creation.

However, the Mishnah in Sanhedrin (37a) says that "Every Jew must say 'the entire world was created just for me!'" In other words, Hashem made the whole universe, just for us to serve Him. His inspiration to create all of the higher and lower worlds, was solely based on the splendor and *kavod* that Hashem would receive from each and every Jew, like the Sages say, "[The Nation of] Yisroel arose in [Hashem's] mind from the beginning (Bereishis Rabbah, A)." In addition, Rashi explains on the first word in the Torah that the purpose of creation was just for Jews to perform Hashem's mitzvos.

Rebbe Nachman, z"tl explains this more in depth. He says that when Hashem thought to create the entire universe as a whole, he first looked at the souls of the Jewish people as a whole. Then, based on the wondrous glory and honor that He saw that the Jewish people would give to His name, he formed all the worlds.

Next, when Hashem thought to make each individual creation – such as a lion, tree or stone – He first examined the incredible splendor and *nachas* that He would receive from each and every individual Jew. Then, based on this splendor, He created all of the specific creations of this world.

Lastly, when Hashem came to complete each creation with all of its unique and precise details – such as limbs, organs, and hairs, etc. – He first looked at the unbelievable joy and pleasure that He would receive from every specific part of each Jew. Then, based on this joy, He completed each creation with all of its amazing details and complexities.

When we take a moment to contemplate this teaching of Rebbe Nachman, we can begin to fathom the immeasurable love that Hashem has for us, and the unbelievable power that we have in changing the world. From here, we see that the Jewish people as a whole have an incredible mission to reveal Hashem's Presence as the Creator of all the worlds. Since, it was specifically for *this purpose* that Hashem thought to make the entire creation!

Not only that, but each and every one of us has our own unique role to play in revealing Hashem in the world, according to the aspect of creation which was inspired by our *shoresh neshamah*. This specific splendor and beauty that we can give to Hashem cannot be accomplished by anyone else in the entire world. Based on the unique qualities that each one of us has, we have our own unique purpose that is extremely vital in bringing the entire creation to an awareness of Hashem.

However, it goes even further. Not only does each one of us play a vital role, rather even each limb, organ, and hair on our bodies reveals Hashem's Presence in an incredibly profound way. When we run to go to shul, we reveal a unique aspect of Hashem's Presence with our legs. When we cover ourselves with a tallis, we reveal a unique aspect of Hashem's Presence with our body. When we wrap tefillin on our arm and place them on our head, we reveal a unique aspect of Hashem's Presence based on those limbs. Even when we simply twist the hair of our *peyos* or run our fingers through our beard, we give Hashem incredible *nachas* and reveal that it was He who created every single hair on all of the creations in the world.

In other words, it is literally in our hands to fulfill the purpose of every physical creation. For example, water has no inherent value to Hashem. But when a Jew takes a cup of it and pours it three times on his right and left hands, the water becomes a means of revealing the *kedushah* of Hashem in the world and pushes away the forces of contamination. Similarly, *rugelach* have no inherent value to Hashem. But when a Jew takes some *rugelach* and says a berachah before and after eating it, he reveals to the world that it is Hashem who creates and sustains the entire world and the *rugelach* as well. That is the entire purpose for the existence of the *rugelach*.

Just by davening *shacharis*, we completely transform the universe.

The same is true when it comes to the primary *avodah* of each and every day: davening *shacharis*. We shouldn't approach the *seder* of *shacharis* as just a random collection of blessings, verses, and prayers, which we say by rote and fulfill our obligations. Rather, we must realize that each section has a unique purpose in rectifying our *neshamah* and the entire universe around us, and by davening *shacharis* each day we are elevating the physical and spiritual worlds to Hashem.

The heavenly angels are waiting patiently for us to start davening (see Zohar, Lech Lecha 90).

Sometimes, we find ourselves sitting and staring blankly at our siddur, daydreaming away until the chazan finally starts *Yishtabach*. What we don't realize is that there are millions upon millions of heavenly angels just waiting for us to open our mouths and say, "*Baruch she'amar ve'haya ha'olam!*" Only then, can the angels begin their praises of Hashem and bless Him for having such a holy nation. When we contemplate this even for a moment, we find the strength to wake up from our inner laziness and sing to Hashem.

When we understand its importance, *korbanos* can actually be very exciting.

When we say *korbanos*, we are lifting sparks of *kedushah* which have fallen and been lost among the contaminated *klipos* due to our sins, and elevate them back to the highest spiritual levels (**see Likutei Halachos, Birkas Hashachar 3:90**). This was the most exalted *avodah* in the Beis HaMikdash, which is now at the tip of our tongue to fulfill. Even though reciting the verses of the *korban tamid* may seem excruciatingly mundane, if we see it in this light, saying them can become very exciting.

By saying *Pesukei d'Zimrah*, we are connecting the physical and spiritual worlds.

After *korbanos*, we say *Pesukei d'Zimrah*, in which we praise Hashem for every aspect of creation. We praise Him for all of the angels, stars, and the sky. We praise Him for all of the trees, birds, and animals. We praise Hashem for making such a holy Jewish people and bringing us close to Him. Even though all of this physical world is seemingly detached from the higher, purely spiritual worlds, through these songs of praise, we reveal that Hashem's presence fills the entire creation and thus we connect the physical to the spiritual in complete unity (see Likutei Halachos, Nesias Kapaim 5:6).

By saying *Yotzer Ohr*, we inspire the angels to praise Hashem.

Then, we say *Birchas Krias Shemah*. Reb Nosson of Breslov, z"tl explains (Likutei Halachos, Birkas Hashachar 5:28) that through our recitation of the brachah of *Yotzer Ohr*, we reveal that all of the angels of Heaven act purely according to Hashem's Divine Will. Therefore, as we're saying the words, we should know the effect we're having in the higher spiritual realms, and imagine the angels repeating after us, "*Kadosh, Kadosh, Kadosh, etc.*"

In *Ahavah Rabbah*, we reveal the ultimate purpose of the world.

Afterwards, in *Ahavah Rabbah*, we express our deepest yearning to do Hashem's will and follow His Torah. Through this prayer, we reveal that the ultimate purpose of this world is our Torah and mitzvos. Amid a world of atheism and *avodah zarah*, we pour out our heart with the desire to be a Jew and serve Hashem. What could be more precious in His eyes?

Through *Krias Shema*, we unify all of creation.

Next, we unify Hashem's name by saying *Krias Shema*. By closing our eyes from all of the brokenness of this world, and proclaiming the oneness of Hashem, we lift up all of creation and return it to its Source. By saying "baruch *Shem*..." we show that Hashem's unity exists even in the darkest and most distant physical and spiritual places (see Likutei Halachos, Maake 4:8).

When we daven *Shemonah Esrei*, we can completely change the order of nature.

Then, we are ready to enter into the *Kodesh HaKadoshim* – Hashem's private chamber – and attach ourselves to Him in the *Shemonah Esrei*. By davening to Hashem to help us achieve our physical and spiritual needs, we reveal the incredible power that each and every Jew has. Through our tefillos, we are able to change the order of nature.

For example, it could be that according to our mazal we're only meant to have a little bit of *parnassah*. However, when we stand before Hashem and daven for a better livelihood, we completely alter the natural order of the universe and change our own destiny as well. From this we see that we have the potential to be even higher than all of Hashem's angels. As pure and holy as they are, they can only do exactly what they are told. We, on the other hand, have the ability to recreate the world together with Hashem through our prayers.

We must also remember that even the seemingly mundane things that we do are incredibly important to Hashem. Just the fact that we refrain from eating until after davening, gives Hashem so much *nachas*. Every morning, we start our day by putting our *neshamah* above our *guf*. Every time we say a berachah, even without so much *kavanah*, the uproar in Heaven is tremendous.

By seeing the importance of our mitzvos, we can find new strength.

When we're able to open our spiritual eyes and wake up our soul to the unbelievable mission that we have in this world, we can find the strength to pull ourselves out of bed. When we see the incredible impact that we have on the entire universe just by davening one *shacharis*, and all the more so when we add the other mitzvos which we do throughout the day, we can find the inspiration to shake off the bonds of sleep and start our day with enthusiasm.

We are no longer dependent on countless cups of coffee and cans of Red-Bull in order to supply a constant flow of caffeine into our bloodstream, since we get such an amazing thrill from serving Hashem. Just being a religious Jew is exciting and enjoyable.

We can find the inspiration to take every single spare moment we have to open a *sefer*. We can find the inspiration to turn off our smartphones and say *Tehillim*. We can find a deep yearning and desire to serve Hashem. Perhaps, we can even find the strength to daven *netz* and wake up for *chatzos*! Each day of our life becomes an incredible opportunity and every second is precious to us.

Even if our *avodah* is mixed with tons of garbage, it is still very important and precious to Hashem.

But sometimes we think, "What real value could my *avodas Hashem* have? Even on a good day I can hardly have any *kavanah* in davening. I can't even sit down to learn more than one Mishnah, and I can only give one *shekel* to *tzedakah*." Nonetheless, we have to know that even the little bit of imperfect things we do for Hashem, are actually sustaining all of creation. Even the little bit of good that's in our *avodah* gives Hashem much pleasure and *nachas*. To understand this better, read the following parable:

One day, the garbage man was feeling a little down. He thought to himself, "What am I really worth? My job is so meaningless. Other people really contribute to society with their work, but what do I do? I just throw away garbage that no one wants anyway. Nobody ever notices what I do or even says thank you to me. In fact, they usually run away when they see me coming. Today, I'm going to sleep in."

And so, the garbage man missed one day. People wondered what had happened, but no one said anything. The garbage man thought, "I knew that no one would care," and so, he missed the next day… And the next day…

Pretty soon, the garbage began piling up. The bins overflowed into the streets and side-walks, and then into peoples' yards. Cars couldn't drive in the streets and no one could walk on the side-walks. People didn't even want to go outside because it smelled so bad. The entire city just shut down.

Finally, after a week, the mayor of the city thought that he should pay a visit to the garbage man. He schlepped through the garbage from his fancy home on the rich side of town, all the way to the slums, and knocked on the garbage man's door.

The garbage man opened up, and was shocked to see the mayor at his door. "What are you doing here, Mr. Mayor?" He asked. "You're so busy and important; what could you possibly have to do with me?"

The Mayor replied, "Don't you see all the garbage all over the place?! Don't you realize that the entire city can't function without you?! Your job may seem menial to you, but without you, our whole society is completely destroyed."

And so, with new enthusiasm, the garbage man went back to work, and cleaned up the city in no time!

So too, it may seem to us like our *avodas Hashem* is very insufficient. Our davening might be so full of thoughts about making money, news and politics, that we feel like we're just taking out the garbage. After speaking *lashon harah* with our tefillin on, we feel like we might as well throw them in the trash.

In addition, it seems like there is no recognition for anything good that we do. It seems that there is no thank you for putting on our tallis and answering to *kaddish* and *kedushah*. We think that Hashem only cares about the *avodah* of the people who are better than us and can actually do something significant in serving Him. We, on the other hand, woke up too late and are too spiritually weak to make a difference. Would it really matter if we took a day off?

However, these thoughts are all just the work of our *yetzer harah* trying to stop us from doing what we can. The reality is that the whole universe depends on the *avodah* of the simple Jew. Just by praying three times a day, we are cleaning this world of countless spiritual *klipos* and contamination. Through every mitzvah that we do, even with its imperfections, we are rectifying the sin of the Tree of Knowledge by choosing to do good. Every moment that we are not transgressing a prohibition, we are getting rid of the forces of evil in the world.

Even if we only make small changes, this has a huge impact on the world.

As lowly as we may seem in our own eyes, we are *mamash* the top priority in Hashem's eyes. It may take time, before we can completely transform our bad habits and wake up with true excitement. Nonetheless, we should be filled with incredible joy for every little bit of success we achieve. If we get up with nine snoozes instead of ten, that's already a reason to celebrate. Even small improvements go a long way towards revealing Hashem's Presence to all of Creation. The more we strengthen our belief in the importance of our mission in this world; the more we will have the strength to jump out of bed and pursue it. With this understanding, we will finally be able to unglue ourselves from our bed and serve Hashem with true joy.

Chapter Two

The Illness: Sometimes, I have good days and I can do avodas Hashem. But other days, I have no inspiration and I don't do anything.

Our lives can often feel like a rollercoaster. One day, week, or month, we rise higher and higher in our spirituality. Sometimes, we even go *really* high. We're happy and inspired to serve Hashem. We're able to wake up early to daven and put *all* our strength into the words of tefillah. We're able to focus during our learning and taste the sweetness of the Torah. We're able to smile when we come home and be patient with our children.

However, when that day, week, or month is over; we feel our momentum petering out, and all of a sudden we take a nose dive into the darkness. We lose our inspiration to get out of bed and we don't feel anything in our davening. Our mind is so dead that we can't make heads or tails of the Gemara and it becomes a comfortable pillow for our morning nap. Our spiritual tank is empty, and we can't find the gas station to fill it up.

In addition, it seems like the world is trying to stop us from doing *avodas Hashem*. Our wife needs our help with countless things and our kids are constantly crying to us for this and that. We hit massive unexpected traffic on our way to shul and our *chavrusah* stops showing up. Every little thing that could go wrong, does go wrong and we have to find a way to fix it.

We wait and hope for the day when we will be able to serve Hashem again, but it seems few and far between. Sometimes, it doesn't happen at all. In the meantime, we have stalled completely and we can barely lift a finger in our learning and davening.

The Rebbe's Prescription: *When you realize that the main thing is your desire to serve Hashem; there are no more bad days. (Based on Likutei Mohoran I, 33, and Sichos HaRan, 14)*

When we take complete responsibility for our success in *avodas Hashem*, we're bound to fall.

Our main mistake in life and *avodas Hashem* is arrogance. When we're able to have a good day of davening and learning; we attribute it to ourselves. We think, "Look at me. *I* was able to wake up early and come to shul before everyone else. *I* was able to daven such a long *Shemoneh Esrei* with so much *kavanah*. *I* was able to get the right *p'shat* in the Tosafos and the Rashba. I did it!" We think that we worked hard and that we earned our accomplishments in *avodas Hashem* all by ourselves!

Inevitably though, a day comes when no matter how hard we try; the gates are closed and we can't get in. We give it our greatest effort, but with no results. The lights are out and we're struggling in the darkness to find the switch, but we're totally unsuccessful. So, we get down on ourselves and we think that we are insufficient. Since we weren't able to serve Hashem today as we did before; we think that our *avodah* is worthless. Then we sink into a depression, since we feel that we can't do anything…

It is only with Hashem's help that we're able to serve Him.

What we don't realize is that in the past, our inspiration to serve Hashem was purely a gift from Above. Hashem opened up the Heavens and let us in. He gave us the physical and spiritual strength to fly in our *avodah*. Certainly, we did our part as well. Without our efforts, even the greatest abundance of Divine assistance wouldn't be able to help us. However, our main source of strength came from Him Himself, as it says in the verse , "Who came before Me, and I will repay him?" And like is says in another verse, "From Your hand, we gave [back] to You."

From here, we see that our success in *avodas Hashem* is completely dependent on Divine assistance. Therefore, when we're having a good day, we should thank and praise Hashem from the bottom of our hearts for His loving-kindness. We should bless Him for giving us the ability to daven with *kavanah* and spend every moment learning His Torah. We should express our gratitude for letting us taste the sweetness of *avodas Hashem*.

And when we hit those days, or even long periods of time, when our *avodah* is freezing cold and we can't find any place to go to warm up; we shouldn't get down on ourselves. We shouldn't feel like we are any worse than we were previously. We shouldn't feel like our davening and learning are any less valuable than before. Even if the actual results we see before our eyes can't compare; nevertheless, this is simply because we weren't given the same Divine assistance that we had on our good days.

Hashem takes away our inspiration, so that we must strengthen our desire for Him.

However, a big question remains: *Why does Hashem take away our inspiration?* The answer is very simple: He wants us to grow. He wants us to build our *ratzon*.

Take the following parable which is said in the name of the Baal Shem Tov, z"tl (see Likutei Halachos, Chadash 5:15):

A little boy is learning how to walk. At first, his father holds his hand with each and every step. He helps his son balance himself and put one foot in front of the other. The son is absolutely thrilled. He thinks this is amazing! He is walking just like his father does. Day after day, the father assists his son and shows him how to walk.

Finally, the day comes when the father decides that his son is ready to try to do it by himself. So, he lets go of his son's hand. The son immediately falls down. Then, he gets back up and tries again; but again, he's unsuccessful. After a third time, the son starts to cry… He doesn't get it. Walking used to be so easy and fun. Now, it seems impossible! What he was able to do yesterday without any effort, is now completely beyond his capability.

Little does he know, however, that every effort that he makes is *so* precious in his father's eyes. His father doesn't care nearly as much about the results, as he does about his son's desire to succeed. Additionally, if he continues to try on his own; then slowly but surely, soon he will be able to walk without any assistance at all… and he will indeed grow up to be like his father.

This is what we're going through with our *avodas Hashem*. For a period of time, especially when we make a new start in our life; things can seem like a walk in the park. We feel spiritually connected and it seems almost instinctual for us to run to learn and do mitzvos. But after that inspiration eventually dies down; we're left sitting on the ground, crying over what we have lost. However, we must understand that those days of emptiness are really opportunities. Those days are a chance for us to build up our own inner strength. On those days, we have an opportunity to grow immensely in our relationship to Hashem and His mitzvos.

How do we do it? We must strengthen our *ratzon*. Since the actual results of our efforts are in Hashem's Hands, as mentioned above, then it's clear what's expected of us: we have to want to serve Him. We have to cultivate inside of ourselves a deep desire for Hashem; to the point that no matter what situation we may find ourselves in both physically and spiritually, we will never give up. We will always yearn to be close to Him and to serve Him with all of our strength.

Even if we're not able to daven with *kavanah*, we shouldn't despair and throw in the towel completely. Rather, we must hold on tightly to our desire to attach ourselves to Hashem in tefillah. We must try to catch a few verses or berachos throughout our *shacharis* and say them from our heart.

If we don't have a clear head to learn *be'iyun*, we shouldn't just go back to sleep. Rather, we must strengthen our *ratzon* for learning, and take out Mishnayos or Mishnah Berurah and do what we can. Although our Torah and *tefillah* don't look anything like they did on our "good old days," nevertheless, this time they are even more important in Hashem's eyes; since now we're showing Him how much we really want to serve Him. Despite our lack of inspiration, we're still giving it everything we've got.

Our main freedom of choice is to *want* to learn Torah and do mitzvos.

This is what Hashem expects from us, and this is why He takes away our inspiration. This is why He gives us a multitude of obstacles, which prevent us from seeing actual results in our *avodas Hashem*. The only reason why He sends us "bad days" – when it seems like there is no way to serve Him with all of our external and internal obstacles that seem to be blocking us – is in order for us to strengthen our desire for *avodas Hashem*. And even if we're not successful in our *avodah* at all; when we're able to build our *ratzon* to serve Him in the face of our obstacles, we give Hashem the greatest *nachas*. Therefore, we must treasure our yearning for Hashem more than all the wealth in the world. We must cherish it even more than all of our concrete achievements in *avodas Hashem*.

Why? As, indeed, this is the only thing that is in our hands. This is our freedom of choice: to never let go of our *ratzon*. This is our main *avodah* in life and this is what will be judged for when we leave this world. *Did we try to do our best even in the face of our obstacles? Did we want to serve Hashem and yearn for Him?* This is what is most important to Him, as our Sages say, "The Compassionate One wants our heart." Certainly, Hashem likes it when we're able to bring our desires into action, and this should always be our goal. However, we must recognize the unbelievable value of our *ratzon*, in and of itself.

If we try our best to do a mitzvah, even if we fail in the end; it's considered as if we accomplished it.

Additionally, our Sages say (Brachos 6a): "One who thought to do a mitzvah but was prevented, it is considered as if he did it." From here, we see the incredible compassion of Hashem. Regardless of the outcome, He takes our desire to serve Him and transforms it into action; as if we actually succeeded in our *avodah*. This may be hard for us to believe; but if Hashem can create the entire Universe from nothing, certainly He can do this as well.

This not only applies when the obstacle which prevents us is external – we got stuck in traffic on the way to a mitzvah, we got sick and couldn't daven, etc. – rather, this is true even if it is our own *yetzer harah* that prevented us. For example, we really wanted to learn a *daf Gemara*. We made the time and we were all ready to go… But then, our mind started to wander into worries about our finances and our kids. We tried our best to push away our thoughts away and start learning; but we were unsuccessful, until we looked at our watch and we had to stop. Nevertheless, it is considered as if we learned that daf!

This is *especially* true, when it comes to davening… We simply cannot judge our success from the amount of *kavanah* we are able to have. Some days, our mind is clear and we're able to focus. Other days, no matter how hard we try, we can't concentrate even on one verse. Perhaps, our *yetzer harah* is dumping buckets full of worries on our head. Or perhaps, he's throwing at us albums of inappropriate images. Or perhaps, we're *so* hungry that all we can think about is bagels and lox!

In the face of such obstacles, any effort we make to daven is huge. If we're able to hold on to our desire to have *kavanah* and continue trying until the end, then we have achieved great success. It is considered as if we davened an extraordinary *Shemoneh Esrei*. We may not have any results to show for it, but we know that in Hashem's eyes; just our *ratzon* alone is invaluable. It is worth more than all the diamonds and gold – i.e. tefillos with *kavanah* – which we achieved without so much effort. We gave our whole heart up to Hashem. It is considered as if we ourselves were a *korban* on His altar (see Sichos HaRan, 12).

> **If we continue to build our *ratzon* and express it in personal prayer to Hashem; we will eventually succeed and see results.**

Additionally, much like the child learning to walk on his own, not only is the desire itself precious to Hashem, but it is also the path for us to eventually be able to be truly strong in our *avodah* and see incredible results, no matter what the circumstances are (see Likutei Mohoran I, 66).

Torah, tefillah, and mitzvos are the most valuable items in the entire universe, so Hashem can't give them away for free. He can't make it easy for us to attach ourselves to His service with incredible love and awe. Rather, we have to earn it. We have to gather enough spiritual money – *kesef* – in order to acquire Hashem's Torah, because *only then* will it really belong to us.

Therefore, Hashem sends us obstacles and He makes it very difficult for us to succeed, in order for us to have to build our spiritual "*kesef*" – in other words "yearning," from the *lashon* of *kisufim* – to overcome the obstacles and acquire His mitzvos. The more valuable the mitzvah, the more "*kesef*" (yearning) we must collect; and in turn, the more obstacles we have to overcome.

So, we shouldn't be discouraged when we encounter countless barriers preventing us from serving Hashem. Since the *avodah* we're trying to get to is so incredibly valuable; it is only through the process of overcoming our barriers that we acquire the necessary desire to get attached to it properly. Indeed, when we're able to be strong in our desire and never let up regardless of our results; then it is only a matter of time until we have the amount we need to attain the mitzvah.

However, in order for us to take that spiritual money and actually purchase the mitzvah – i.e. bring our desires into action – we must express our *ratzon* in words. We must transform our deep desire to serve Hashem into our own unique tefillah. We must take our longing to find inspiration in our *avodah* and turn it into a personal prayer to the Master of the Universe.

This step is absolutely crucial in bringing our *ratzon* into action. By expressing our desires to Hashem and asking for His help; we accomplish two important things. Firstly, we are opening ourselves up to receive help from Heaven to overcome our struggles. Without this, there is no way for us to rise above our obstacles. Our main freedom of choice is to choose *not* to try to do everything on our own: Rather, we must recognize our dependence on the Creator and reach out to Him for help.

Secondly, through expressing our desire to change in words, we are bringing our holy *ratzonos* from the realm of just potential into reality. Our ideas don't remain stuck in our heads; rather they come into a physical existence. This can be better understood through the science of sound, where we know that every sound creates waves that travel through the air .Indeed similarly, by speaking out our deepest yearnings to be close to Hashem; we are sending positive energy throughout our body and the world. This is much like when a stone is dropped in water, which causes waves to spread out in all directions. Therefore, with our speech we can bridge the gap between our thoughts, which are metaphysical, and our actions which are physical. Once we're able to transform our desire for teshuvah from thought into speech; we are exponentially closer to bringing it into action.

Through this, we will eventually see our success before our own eyes. We will see that through our deep *ratzon* to serve Hashem we've grown so much and we've reached a higher level. However, this time, instead of our success being a present from the Almighty, it is now ours. We earned it, so to speak, not through the merit of our actions, rather through the sincerity of our desire.

By constantly yearning for Hashem we will be able to hold on throughout all of the difficulties of life. There will no longer be any more "bad" days, since even if we're not able to serve Hashem like we aspire to, our *ratzon* is unbreakable. We are so strong and sturdy like iron that all the heaviest winds in the world can't knock us over. We know that it is this *ratzon* which Hashem treasures more than anything else, and through strengthening our deepest desire to serve Him, we will be able to overcome all of our obstacles.

Chapter Three

The Illness: It seems like there is an alien in my mind who is sending my thoughts on a rollercoaster out of my control.

Sometimes, it appears to us like there is an alien inside our head who's controlling our thoughts and trying to make us completely nuts. He turns our mind around in circles, sending us from one worry to the next. It seems like there is an endless amount of bad things that could potentially happen to us, and we are obligated by our alien to be afraid of them all. Very often we know that this is ridiculous, but we still can't stop the alien.

He also sends us thoughts about making money. We imagine for hours at a time, all the scenarios in which we can become multimillionaires. He sends us lustful thoughts and drags us into really low places. He'll make us think about delicious foods which we have to eat immediately. He spins us on a rollercoaster of physical desires, throwing us around from one nose dive to the next!

The alien especially loves to make it impossible for us to daven. Our tefillah is his favorite time to make our mind into complete chaos. We wish that we could just hit the brakes and stop the circus; but it's going way too fast and out of control. We feel like we have absolutely no capability to shut him up or kick him out… We feel like slaves.

The Rebbe's Prescription: Don't stop to think! Just keep doing avodas Hashem, and eventually the alien will go away. (Based on Likutei Mohoran I, 72)

When we try to fight with our foreign thoughts, we only give them more strength.

When we're struggling to control our mind, very often our natural instinct is to try to push away our negative thoughts. For example, when we can't stop ourselves from worrying about our debt, and our mind is running around with all kinds of fear and dread; we instinctively try to fight these thoughts head-on. Sometimes, we try to tell them to shut up or we try to force them out of our mind. Sometimes, we try to answer some of our doubts with potential solutions, in the hope that this will get them to go away. Other times, we try to get rid of them by resolving them with logic and reason. We tell them that it doesn't help to go over these things in our head, and nothing productive will come from it. Worrying has never helped improve our finances. Other times, we try to overcome them by strengthening our faith and telling them that Hashem will take care of us and give us what we need.

But these tactics very rarely work. When we try to combat our negative thoughts head-on by forcing them out or answering them; they simply get stronger and stronger. The more that we come up with counter-attacks to get rid of them; they respond by taking over our mind even more. They tell us, "Do you really think that Hashem is going to provide for you? You don't have so much faith. Who are you kidding? You know that you need to think really hard to come up with a way to pay off your loans. How else is it going to happen? Get back to work!"

As a result, we lose the battle and end up spending most of our lives in "la-la land," unable to focus on our davening and unable to sit down and concentrate on a Gemara.

We must completely ignore our alien and try to attach our thoughts to whatever *avodah* we're occupied with.

However, Rebbe Nachman has the answer: He explains that when we try to fight with our bad thoughts, we are only giving them fuel for their fire. It's similar to when a child is being teased by a bully, and the child gets upset and tries to make fun of him back. This only spurs the bully on to do him more harm. It gets the bully even more excited; since he sees that he's able to hurt him with his words. *What should the child do instead?* He shouldn't pay attention to him at all. He should pretend like the bully doesn't exist. Even if the bully may continue to tease him time after time; when the bully sees that he's unable to make the child upset, he will eventually leave him alone completely.

This is exactly the way we must react to our alien. We must simply turn our back to him and continue doing what we're doing. For example, if we're in the middle of davening, we should just keep going. We should continue saying the words and trying to focus on their meaning. Even if we're unable to concentrate because the alien won't leave us alone; nevertheless we must pay absolutely no attention to him and just keep trying to daven.

When someone is trying to escape his enemy, if he looks back to see how close his enemy is to him; this inspires his enemy to continue tracking him down. The same is true with our alien. Therefore, we should run away and not look back. We should try not to care at all about any of the thoughts he throws at us. We should try not to be affected by the crazy things that are going through our head.

Even if we don't succeed in having any *kavanah* whatsoever; nevertheless we did everything that we could. We tried our best to escape him, and Hashem sees our efforts and gets incredible *nachas* from us. At the end of the day, we really need Divine assistance to succeed in serving Hashem, especially when it comes to tefillah. Therefore, we should lift our eyes to Heaven, and pray for Hashem's help. But at the same time, we should be extremely pleased with our efforts to daven with *kavanah*.

If we stubbornly refuse to engage with our bad thoughts; they will eventually leave us alone.

Also, we must know that if we continue to disregard our foreign thoughts; eventually they will go away, just like the bully. After a while, our alien will see that he's unable to make us upset and can't prevent us from serving Hashem, and so he will stop bothering us.

However, it may take a while. We may have to ignore our bad thoughts time after time. We may have to be extremely stubborn, and even though it seems like we're not making any progress… we must believe that each time we ignore our alien, we're chipping away at his strength. Each time, we're weakening his resolve a little bit. It could take fifty times, or it could take a hundred or even a thousand times, but eventually, he will stop coming by. And in the meantime, we're not losing anything. On the contrary, Hashem loves our stubbornness, and He appreciates our strong desire to serve Him with a pure mind – more than anything else in the world.

We should make use of this tactic whenever we lose control of our thoughts. No matter what situation we're in, we must simply continue with what we're doing. We shouldn't stop even for a second to try to entertain our alien's thoughts. We shouldn't stop even for a second to try and push them away…

Rather, if we're learning Torah we must simply force ourselves to keep reading the words. We must try our best to keep our eyes on the page and keep our thoughts in the *sefer* we're studying. If we're at work, we must try to concentrate on whatever task we're doing and not look back. Our foreign thoughts probably won't leave us alone right away. However, if we're very stubborn and we continue to ignore them; they will eventually stop bothering us.

Since it is impossible to have two thoughts in our mind at one time; all we have to do is put something else in our head.

To understand this piece of advice on a deeper level, Rebbe Nachman explains why it is so effective. Even though when our head is spinning out of control, it may seem to us that multiple thoughts are coming simultaneously into our mind, this is not true. Our mind only has the ability to think of one thing at a time. It's only because our thoughts are coming so quickly one after the other without any pause or respite, that it appears to us that they are simultaneous (see Likutei Mohoran I, 233).

Once we understand this, the path of escape from our negative thoughts is very clear: we must simply think about something else! Since it is impossible to have two thoughts in our mind at one time, all we have to do is attach our mind to another subject and our foreign thoughts will be immediately usurped. All we have to do is pick up a *sefer*, recite *tehillim*, think about this week's parashah, or even read a newspaper, and we can eliminate the alien from our head.

We should approach our initial foreign thoughts as opportunities to do teshuvah.

We must also know that even if we have really bad thoughts coming into our head over and over again, we should never get discouraged and never feel like a failure. Our Sages say (Yuma 86b) that the only way to do teshuvah is by going back to the same situation in which we sinned and choosing to do the right thing. Rebbe Nachman explains that this doesn't just mean the same physical place and circumstances as before, rather even if in our mind, we find ourselves in the same situation where we sinned; this is also an opportunity to fix our previous transgressions (see Likutei Mohoran I, 27 towards the end).

Therefore, when foreign thoughts are coming into our head, we shouldn't get down on ourselves at all! Rather, we should completely turn the tables on our alien and approach our negative thoughts as opportunities. Hashem allows our alien to bother us so much, in order to give us many chances to do teshuvah. Instead of having to go back to the same places where we sinned; we can rectify everything in our own mind by simply choosing not to think bad thoughts and attaching our mind to other things, as discussed before.

In other words, we are not held accountable for the initial foreign thought which pops into our head. This is the work of the alien who's trying to destroy us, and on a deeper level, it is the work of Hashem who is trying to help us fix our mistakes. Therefore, we should in no way feel any remorse about this initial thought. Nevertheless, we must be careful not to get sucked into the initial thought and continue thinking about it. For this, we are held accountable. HaKadosh Baruch Hu sees every single thought that we have, and if we continue to engage in our bad thoughts, even for a little while, it is harmful to our neshamah and not praiseworthy in His eyes.

Rather, we should immediately occupy ourselves with something else; whether it's Torah, or tefillah, or even secular things which will take our mind off of our bad thoughts. When we're able to do so, we are also in the process of fixing our previous mistakes and purifying ourselves of sin.

The struggle with our alien is much easier if we run away from him, immediately, without hesitation.

Additionally, there is another reason why it is pertinent that we don't engage in our foreign thoughts even for one moment. Very often, our alien tricks us by telling us that it's not so bad if we worry just for a little bit about the future, or if we have inappropriate thoughts just for a little while. He tries to convince us to indulge in his ideas for a moment or two, with a guarantee that once the moment is over… he will let us go back to our right mind.

However, we must be extremely careful of this plot; because once we're in the alien's hands, he simply won't let us go. After he's fooled us into indulging in his thoughts even for a split second, then it is increasingly harder to ignore him and attach our mind to something else. When we make one tiny misstep into his territory; then he grabs a hold of us and throws us down into his prison, and locks us up with a ball and chain. From one bad thought, we find ourselves on a rollercoaster of worse thoughts that can spin around us for hours.

Therefore, it is very important that we "nip him in the bud," and don't give in to our alien one inch! We must immediately distract ourselves without letting him get one word in. Although it is still difficult to turn away from our alien, especially if we're accustomed to having him as our regular guest; nevertheless it is much easier to ignore him if we can avoid any interaction to begin with. It is easier for us to pretend like he doesn't exist, before we've started talking to him.

If we fall into his hands, we shouldn't get depressed. Rather, we should grab the reins and pull our mind back.

Nevertheless, even if we do get dragged down into our alien's trap, we still shouldn't get down on ourselves. Sadness is our alien's main fuel, and it will only cause us to fall even further. Instead, we must gather all the spiritual strength we can possibly find, and grab our mind out of the gutter and put it directly into something kosher. We must take the reins of the horse with all the force we have, and turn him to a different direction.

Every single attempt that we make to purify our mind gives Hashem a lot of *nachas*.

We must know that every attempt that we make to escape our foreign thoughts is incredibly valuable to Hashem. Rebbe Nachman compares the struggle between our good thoughts and bad thoughts like an organized fight between a pure animal and a contaminated one; similar to what the Romans used to observe as sport in their stadiums. Whenever, the pure animal takes charge the crowd goes wild and cheers. It gives them so much enjoyment to see their favorite side winning. So too, we have both pure and contaminated animals – thoughts – inside of our head. Hashem observes the struggle between them and He gets unbelievable *nachas* with every attempt that we make to cause the pure thoughts to win (see Likutei Mohoran I, 233).

In fact, this is the purpose of the Creation of the World: for us to choose to do good. This is obviously true about our speech and actions; but, it is also true about our thoughts. Every time that we think only about positive, holy things *mamash* brings the entire world closer to its completion. Every time we just make an effort to ignore our foreign thoughts; we are bringing the entire universe closer to perfection.

Chapter Four

The Illness: Day after day passes me by and I'm not able to accomplish anything in my learning.

For many of us, it seems like we're frozen in time. We have our routine — we go to shul and daven every day; we work and spend time with our families — however, we find that we're unable to attach ourselves to learning on a regular basis. When we look back at the previous week, month, or year; it seems like we're stuck in one place and we haven't progressed at all in our Torah studies.

Similarly, even for those of us who are learning in kollel or yeshivah every day, we often feel like time is slipping through our fingers. We end up spending much of our seder taking coffee or cigarette breaks, playing with or talking on our phones, or just schmoozing with our *chavrusah*. And when our *chavrusah* doesn't show up, we end up taking a long morning nap.

We count down the minutes until kollel is over and we can be free from our obligation to learn. All the more so do we get excited when the *zman* is finally over and we can take a vacation.

So, whether we're working or sitting in the *beis midrash*, time flies… The years pass by before our eyes, and it seems like we're unable to move forward and accomplish anything.

The Rebbe's Prescription: By focusing on one day at a time and learning small daily portions, you will see incredible progress. (Based on Likutei Mohoran I, 272)

Because of all of our problems and distractions, it seems like today is not a day for learning.

When it comes to attaching ourselves to learning and *avodas Hashem* with *deveikus*; there are two constant obstacles we face. The first one is that every single day– almost without fail – we are confronted with difficulties that distract us and take us away from serving Hashem: One day it's too hot in shul... Another day, our back hurts and we can't sit comfortably. The next day, we get a call from our debt collector and our wife screams at us to get a better job... Another day, we have to take our kid to a doctor's appointment and we get stuck in traffic...

Additionally, we have our own internal distractions that take us away from *avodas Hashem:* Sometimes, we spend an entire day worrying about paying rent the next day, or we're anxious about a new and important business deal... Some days, we wake up feeling depressed and we can't get out of bed. ..Other days, we can't stop thinking about a mistake we made the day before and we drown in our guilt...

Due to these problems and distractions, it appears to us like today is just not a day for *avodas Hashem*. Maybe tomorrow, we won't have such problems to deal with and we'll be able to focus on our learning; but right now, it is simply impossible for us to put our head into a Gemara.

So, we spend today trying to alleviate ourselves of our suffering, with the hope that the next day everything will go smoothly and we'll have the *yishuv hadaas* to serve Hashem. However, the next day comes... and we're *still* dealing with the same old problem or a new, unexpected one has cropped up. So we, once again, lose a day of learning trying to resolve the difficulties of our lives. This is the first obstacle.

We feel so overwhelmed by the length and difficulty of a *sefer* to even begin studying it.

The second obstacle is that when we want to start learning a new *sefer* or *masechtah*, we sometimes feel very overwhelmed by its length, depth, and difficulty. We feel like we have to commit so many hours to learning the *sefer* in order to finish it, that we couldn't possibly succeed. It feels like a heavy burden over our heads which we will never be able to carry. So, we give up immediately and completely despair of ever being able to achieve anything challenging in our learning and *avodas Hashem*.

We must remind ourselves that *today* we have a chance to make millions!

Rebbe Nachman teaches us that there is one solution to both of these issues: "*hayom* – today!" To overcome the first obstacle, we must tell ourselves that *today* will never come again. If we don't take the opportunity that we have to serve Hashem right now in this moment; we will never be able to get it back. Tomorrow, we will have more opportunities; but there is no way to replace what we missed today.

In other words, time is extremely precious! Time is spiritual money, which is worth infinitely more than all the wealth of This World. Money, at best, is only good for us while we're alive on earth, but Torah and mitzvos are invaluable treasures for us in This World and, all the more so, in the Next One. They give our lives a purpose and bring us true happiness, and needless to say, they are the only wealth which remains with us after we pass away.

Indeed, every single moment of our lives we have a chance to open up a *sefer* and make millions, even billions of dollars. *How do we respond?* "My back hurts. It's too hot. How can I pay off my debt?" Does this make any sense at all?!

If Donald Trump came knocking on our door with a suitcase full of one-hundred-dollar bills; would we tell him the same thing? What if he came every single day? What if he was constantly chasing us down with a check for the value of his net worth?

Certainly, all of our obstacles would pale in comparison to the benefit we could get by simply letting him in. It would not be difficult for us to put our problems and distractions on hold for a while, in order to acquire the entire Trump estate.

This is what is in our hands and at the tip of our tongues every single day of our lives, and so much more…

So, we must put all of our problems on hold… We must make sure that nothing can get in our way of our *avodas Hashem* and our productivity in learning. We can't let any of the distractions of This World prevent us from getting to the Next One.

The Zohar HaKadosh says (Parashas Nasso, 123) that every day has "good" hidden inside of it. However, this "good" is surrounded on all sides by a wall of snakes, scorpions, and other frightening creatures. Nevertheless, if we ourselves are "good," then the creatures must open up the gates for us to enter and receive the goodness of that day.

Rebbe Nachman explains that the "good" that we're looking for is the Torah. Every day, we have an opportunity to attach ourselves to learning and taste the sweetness of *avodas Hashem*. However, there is a barrier of distracting thoughts and feelings – i.e. harmful creatures – which is keeping us out. Nevertheless, if we really want to receive "good" and we build up our desire to reach it; we will be able to pass over all the obstacles and have a "good" day of learning (see Likutei Mohoran I, 84).

Therefore, no matter what challenges we're being faced with both from the outside world as well as our own emotional and psychological struggles; we must remind ourselves that, nevertheless, we must break through them all and make today a productive day of *avodas Hashem*.

By focusing on one day at a time, we can easily accomplish great things.

The concept of *"hayom"* helps us to overcome the second obstacle as well. When we think about how many days or years it is going to take us to finish a *sefer*, that *sefer* becomes a very heavy burden which we simply cannot carry. Therefore, instead of thinking about the future; we should choose a small amount of that *sefer* to learn daily as a realistic goal for us, and make sure to fulfill that goal. Then, when the next day comes, we should learn the next small portion of the *sefer*, according to whatever amount we prescribed for ourselves. So too, we should take it one day at a time and persevere in continuing to meet our goals.

The classic example of this is the *daf hayomi*. If we were to focus on the fact that it will take us seven and half years to finish the Talmud Bavli, we would almost immediately give up. How could we keep up with the *daf* for so long? What would we do on Erev Shabbos, Shabbos, and Yom Tov, when we have hardly any time at all? Clearly, this train of thought would prevent us from ever starting out.

However, when we take it one day at a time, it's not so bad. When we're able to focus only on today, we can relieve ourselves of the heavy burden of seven and a half years. All that we have to do right now is one *daf* and that is manageable for us. Sure, we're all very busy juggling numerous spiritual and physical obligations each day; but nevertheless, for just one day, we could find some time to do the *daf*. So, we learn the *daf* for that day. Then, when the next day comes, we focus only on that day and "squeeze in" another *daf*. We continue like this day after day…

And even on certain days when we have other mitzvos and really important things to do, and it may seem to us that it's just not possible to sit down and learn; nevertheless, we cannot use this as an excuse. Rather, we must grab every moment we can in between our other mitzvos and pressing obligations to open a *sefer* and do what we can. If we strengthen our *ratzon* to not pay attention to all of our unnecessary distractions, we can still fit in a lot of time here and there.

Nevertheless, if we have a day in which we were so overwhelmed that we couldn't find time to learn, or perhaps we fell into depression for a day, week, or month, and we missed the *daf*; even so, we should never give up! Instead, we should forget about our disappointments and lost opportunities and jump right back in the next day. And with Hashem's help, we will eventually be able to find extra time to make up the pages that we missed.

Then, before we know it, two months have passed and we're already making a *siyum*. A year later we've already finished a number of *masechtahs*. Pretty soon, time flies and it's seven and a half years later and we've finished all of Shas!

Was it hard? For sure, there were some days when it was really challenging. But overall, it wasn't "seven and a half years," it was "one day." Today, then the next day, and then the next...

Through this, we come to truly enjoy learning.

In addition to helping us accomplish a lot in our Torah study, there is another incredible benefit to focusing on one day at a time: we come to enjoy learning! For many of us, Torah feels like an obligation that we must fulfill before we can do the other things that we really enjoy. When we're in yeshivah or kollel, we count down the minutes until the end of morning seder and the days until *bein hazmanim*. All the more so, is it hard for us to look forward to learning when our main occupation is working, and we have to wake up early or stay up late in order to make time to open a *sefer*.

This is because our relationship to Torah is somewhat unstable. Some days we're on, and some days we're off. Some of the time we're less distracted and we're able to focus on our studies, and other days our mind is wandering, or we're falling asleep, or perhaps we don't even show up to shul.

If we were to propose such an agreement to our spouse, it is clear that with such a weak commitment, our relationship would not be enjoyable and probably wouldn't last very long at all. So too with our attachment to Torah – which our Sages compare to a husband's engagement to his wife – if we are inconsistent, we will almost never feel true inspiration and joy in our learning.

However, by making a commitment to learn even a small portion of a *sefer* every day; we become "married" to that *sefer*. We're in it for good – seven days a week, three hundred and sixty-five days a year. Through this, our learning truly becomes a part of us... We begin to think about our *sefer* even during other parts of the day, when we're not studying Torah. We begin to find hints to what we're learning through the events which take place around us.

Just like a good marriage, it doesn't feel like an obligation. Rather, it feels like an integral part of our daily life which we couldn't live without. Just like we eat breakfast, lunch, and dinner every day; so too, we eat three delicious meals of Gemara, Halachah, and Chassidus.

Additionally, the more we're able to commit ourselves to daily learning and focus only on today's *avodah*; the more we can achieve true *yishuv hadaas*. By having a regular *limud*, we can accustom ourselves to forget about all of our worries about tomorrow and our guilt over yesterday, and just sit and learn.

The result of this is incredible! Not only are we able to accomplish so much more than we thought we ever could; rather we're even able to taste the true sweetness of the Torah on a regular basis.

Every single *sefer* has a specific aspect of Hashem's sechel, which is meant to engage our mind in a unique and enjoyable way. The reason why we often don't experience the brilliance of these *sechalim* is because our mind is mixed up with distracting thoughts.

However, once we have a clear head, just by opening a book and reading the words; we naturally experience the sweetness of our *sechel* being connected to the Master of the Universe. Indeed, our learning becomes more enjoyable when we attach ourselves to it day after day and accustom ourselves to focusing our thoughts.

We must remember that each one of us has a *neshamah* that is thirsting for the Torah. Even if we don't experience such a strong desire to learn; we must know that our soul is a letter in Torah, and underneath all our problems and distractions, that letter is deeply yearning to be attached to its Source. The more we accustom ourselves to learning on a regular basis; the more we feel that connection to our Source and truly enjoy our studies.

Through a constant attachment to Torah, we can live beyond the boundaries of time.

Rebbe Nachman describes this daily attachment to learning and *avodas Hashem* as being "above time" (see Likutei Mohoran II, 62 and Likutei Halachos, Matana 5:70). In general, we think of seventy years as a long period of time. We experience time passing very slowly; so it seems like it takes a while for a lifetime to be complete. However, this is only because of our lack of "*daas* – awareness of Hashem." The truth is that the higher the level of awareness that we have; the more we see that time is really flying by very quickly. The clock doesn't stop even for a second. A moment comes and goes, in the blink of an eye. Sometimes, when we look back ten or twenty years, we get a sense of how quickly time has passed. But at any given moment, it seems to most of us that time is dragging slowly along.

Rebbe Nachman helps us understand this idea by using sleep as an example. When we go to sleep and fall into a dreamlike state, it could seem to us like we're living an entire lifetime of seventy years. In our dream, we experience countless things throughout the course of many decades. However, when we wake up and look at the clock; we realize that we just took a fifteen minute nap!

So, why did it seem like such a long time? The answer is that when we were asleep, our level of awareness was only a minute fraction of what it is when we are awake. Thus, it appeared to us like fifteen minutes was seventy years. When we woke up, however, it was clear that only a short period of time really passed. Nevertheless, even in our waking state of consciousness, seventy real years still seems like a really long time. But once again, this is only due to our lack of awareness.

However, when we're able to attach ourselves to learning and *avodas Hashem* every moment that we can; we begin to experience time in a completely different way. Our entire life becomes like one day, and on a higher level, like one moment, since all that exists in our consciousness is the current moment that we're in.

We can taste the awareness of Mashiach and do complete teshuvah.

This level of awareness is an aspect of Mashiach. Even though Mashiach's soul has existed since the beginning of Creation, when the right time will arrive for him to redeem us – *speedily and in our days, amen!* – Hashem will tell Mashiach (*Tehillim* 2), "Today, I have given birth to you." This is because Mashiach's level of *daas* is so great – that despite the incredible amount of things that have happened throughout the course of history – to him, it is all like one day.

The amazing thing is that we also have the ability to tap into this awareness and bring Mashiach today! In *maseches Sanhedrin* (98b), our Sages recount the story of when R' Yehoshua ben Levi went to bring Mashiach. Once R' Yehoshua ben Levi found him, he asked Mashiach when he was going to come, Mashiach responded to him with this verse (*Tehillim* 95): "Today! ...if [the Jewish people] listen to [Hashem's] voice."

From here, we see the incredible power we have in our hands. Simply by taking it one day at a time and listening to Hashem's Voice by filling each day with learning and *avodas Hashem*; we can bring the ultimate Redemption. We can attach ourselves to an aspect of Mashiach's elevated consciousness which is beyond the boundaries of time.

This is the main teshuvah that we must do in our lives, like Rebbe Eliezer says in *maseches Shabbos* (153a), "Do teshuva 'one day' before you die." Upon hearing this, Rebbe Eliezer's students asked him, "How do we know when the last day of our life will be?" Rebbe Eliezer responded, "All the more so that we must do teshuvah every day, since perhaps we may pass away tomorrow. Thus, we will do teshuva every single day."

The great depth of this statement of the Sages is that we must take our lives one day at a time. We must try to focus only on what we can accomplish today, at this very moment. Through this, we can fly in our learning and achieve the greatest levels in *avodas Hashem*. Through this, we can attach ourselves to our Creator and be in a constant state of teshuvah (see Likutei Mohoran II, 79).

Additional pieces of advice in order to strengthen our connection to Torah (based on Sichos HaRan, 76).

In order to achieve this goal and attach ourselves to learning with a constant *deveikus*, Rebbe Nachman gives us a number of additional pieces of advice. As was mentioned before, we should try to take on a portion of a *sefer* – such as a *daf Gemara*, two Mishnayos, an *amud* of *Mishnah Berurah*, or a page of Zohar, etc. – and learn the same amount every day.

We each should assess for ourselves individually how many of these regular portions we can take on and which *sefarim* we would like to learn; without becoming overwhelmed and creating stress in our lives. It is best to start with an amount of daily learning which is easy to accomplish; then, if we find that we can do more, add on extra afterwards.

We shouldn't approach daily portions as just fulfilling obligations; rather we should see them like a tray of delicious desserts. First, we take a few bites of Chumash with Rashi, then some Halachah, then some Gemara, Chassidus, Arizal, etc. Ideally, we would like to taste daily as many desserts as possible; but at the same time, we must recognize our capabilities and only take on what we can handle.

We should try to learn quickly and not get stuck trying to resolve our *kashes*.

When we're studying our daily portions, Rebbe Nachman recommends learning *bekiyus* and moving as quickly as we can. He says that we should read the words on the page out loud and try to understand the simple meaning (*pashut peshat*) of the Torah we're learning. We should do our best not to ask *kashes*; especially if the *kashe* is based on another section of the Torah which is not mentioned on the page we're studying.

Additionally, Rebbe Nachman says that if we get stuck for more than a little while and we can't understand something; we should just keep going… We should not waste time going over and over the passage which is difficult for us, since more often than not, our confusion will be cleared up by another passage later on in the *sefer*. Indeed, even if this does not become clearer, by becoming accustomed to learning quickly, we will be able to finish the entire *sefer* and then begin it again. Certainly, the second time around, we will have a much deeper understanding and many of our uncertainties will be easier to grasp.

Nevertheless, even if we never clarify our confusion; Rebbe Nachman says that in the Next World we will understand every piece of Torah that we learned in This World. So, by going further in our studies, we will acquire much more knowledge when we go to Heaven, which is obviously our primary concern.

By learning *bekiyus*, we can get the big picture and achieve a deep understanding.

This is one of the reasons that Rebbe Nachman says our main *limud* should be *bekiyus*. He explains that, although it is good to learn a small amount in-depth (*be'iyun*) every day; nevertheless, if we focus too much on the details of one section – not only are we unable to cover lots of ground and learn many *sefarim* – we also become lacking in the ability to understand the section we are concentrating on.

On the other hand, when we learn quickly, we have the time to complete the entire *sefer* and many others as well. Then, after we finish, we can start over and learn the *sefer* again. Each time we go over the *sefer*, we get a deeper understanding, until after a number of times, G-d willing, we will know the entire *sefer* in depth.

Since *bekiyus* requires less concentration, it is more accessible to us on a daily basis.

Another reason that our primary *limud* should be *bekiyus* is to make sure that we're constantly attached to learning. As explained above, we have many internal and external obstacles which prevent us from sitting down and learning on a daily basis. Unfortunately, as the generations continue to decline spiritually; it is all to common that these obstacles become too difficult for us to overcome and we end up with many days that are empty of Torah.

While learning *be'iyun* is very important and gives Hashem great *nachas*, it requires a certain level of clarity of mind which many of us are currently lacking. With all of our problems and distractions, we simply can't focus hard enough to be successful at learning *be'iyun*. So, we may end up wasting precious time in the *beis midrash* not really accomplishing anything.

On the other hand, learning *bekiyus* requires much less deep concentration, and is much more accessible to us on a regular basis. Even if we're tired or confused and our mind is not able to grasp complicated concepts; we can still manage to understand the basic meaning of a Gemara with Rashi.

Even if we find that we simply don't have the time or ability to focus and learn a Gemara with Rashi, we can open an ArtScroll translation and read through the *daf*. Even if we *still* find that this is too hard, we can try learning Mishnayos or Chumash with Rashi. And even if we don't have the attention span to sit in front of a *sefer* and learn at all; we don't need to throw in the towel and give up! Nowadays, there are countless *shiurim* available to us on almost any *sefer* that we would like to learn. So we can just put on our headphones and connect our mind to the Torah, whenever we have a free moment.

Indeed, by focusing on the simple understanding of the Torah and learning *bekiyus*, we can attach ourselves to the learning throughout our day, even if we're physically and spiritually weak.

Rebbe Nachman's method of learning is useful even for those of us who are in kollel.

This method of Torah study is also useful for those of us sitting in kollel every day. Even though we are studying in kollel, if we look honestly at how much time our mind is actually involved in learning, many of us will see that we're not engaged in the Torah for long periods of time. We end up schmoozing with our *chavrusah*, talking on our phone, day-dreaming, or even falling asleep. Therefore, it may be that we're better off spending our time learning daily portions *bekiyus* to ensure that we're attached to the Torah every single day of our lives.

If this is not true and we are able to sit for hours learning *be'iyun*, then great! The ultimate goal is that we should be constantly connected to the Torah. So, if we truly prefer learning *be'iyun* and we're able to concentrate for long periods of time, then there is no reason to stop. Nevertheless, even for those of us learning hours a day *be'iyun*, it is still important to have regular daily portions of *bekiyus* in order to get a broader understanding and cover more ground. As discussed before, if we look hard enough, we can always find time to do so, in between and around our kollel obligations.

Chavrusah or no *chavrusah*, we must attach ourselves to learning.

Another valuable reason that Rebbe Nachman says that our learning should be focused on daily portions is because it is not necessary for us to have a *chavrusah* to study them. Very often, many of us struggle to find a *chavrusah* who shows up on time and has the compatible *middos* to work well together with us. As a joke, it is said that it is almost as hard as finding a *shidduch!* So, we waste time waiting for and trying to find the right one.

Additionally, even if we already have a good *chavrusah*, sometimes he's sick and doesn't show up… Or maybe, he has an appointment and has to come late or leave early… Because of this, we end up losing countless hours of learning.

Of course, the solution is not to do away with *chavrusahs* altogether… Learning Torah with another Jew is an invaluable tradition which helps us get a deeper understanding of our studies. Rather, the answer to the problem is that we shouldn't be dependent on our *chavrusah*. This means that whether he shows up or not, we must attach ourselves to our *sefer*. Even if he falls asleep, we must keep a constant connection to Torah.

For this reason, it is imperative that we have daily portions which we learn by ourselves. As explained before, our *bekiyus* learning does not require in-depth analysis; so, we don't need someone else to help us clarify our *kashes* with. Through this, we create our own independent relationship with learning which we can maintain whether we have a *chavrusah* or not.

Our goal is to travel the entire world of Torah, one day at a time.

To help us understand our relationship to learning, Rebbe Nachman gives the following comparison (Sichos HaRan, 28). Among the upper-class non-Jews, it is very popular to boast about all the countries that one has visited and all the different cultures one has experienced. It is a great virtue to have travelled the world and to be well-versed in numerous languages. *Lehavdil*, we should approach learning Torah in a similar way. We should have a strong desire to see all the holy *sefarim* from beginning to end and be well-versed in their subjects. We should approach learning as if we're gathering invaluable information from numerous places in the Torah. Of course, it is not in order to brag to others like the *goyim* do. Instead, it is in order to understand all of Hashem's teachings and be able to attach ourselves to Him on a constant basis.

Through this, we can completely transform our relationship to learning and *avodas Hashem*. Every single day of our lives can be unbelievably productive, filled with Torah and mitzvos from beginning until the end. Then, after years have passed, we will be able to look back… and see how far we've come and how much we've accomplished. We'll be able to see how much we've elevated ourselves beyond the boundaries of time, by focusing only on filling each moment with learning and *avodas Hashem*. Through this, with Hashem's help, we'll be able to achieve true teshuvah and closeness to our Creator.

Chapter Five

The Illness: No matter how many layers I put on, my avodas Hashem still feels freezing cold.

We all know the feeling of being outside in absolutely frigid weather. The wind whips about mercilessly and the temperature is below zero; it seems there is no way to escape the cold. If we are there for too long, it seeps into our bones and leaves us feeling lifeless. So, we run inside to warm up and renew our strength.

The problem is that even in a well-heated building, we can't avoid the frost. Even though our body is warm, our *neshamah* feels cold. It has been "outside" for so long – lost in the desires and distractions of this world – that it has become numb from the spiritual ice and snow.

The result of this is that we don't feel anything in *avodas Hashem*. When we say berachos, we don't feel joy and gratitude. When we wrap ourselves in our holy tallis, we don't feel the warmth of its *kedushah*. When we put on our tefillin, we don't feel the awesome *deveikus* of Hashem's name on our head. When we daven, we don't feel the incredible fire of the words of Dovid HaMelech, and the inspiration of the holy prayers of the Sages.

Everything is just flat. They say in the hospital that when the heart monitor reads one long straight line it's bad news, G-d forbid. For us, our physical heart is beating just fine, but spiritually we feel lifeless. We're living in a Gehinnom of snow and ice, with no place to find warmth.

So, we continue to go through the motions and follow halachah. But something is missing deep down inside: the spark of inspiration – that true love and awe of Hashem – is lacking from our *avodah*.

The Rebbe's Prescription: By living with the awareness that Hashem is *mamash* with you, you can find a spark in your avodah. (Based on Likutei Mohoran I, 62:2)

Even though we know that Hashem is everywhere, we struggle to live with this reality.

The popular children's book says: Hashem is here, Hashem is there, Hashem is truly everywhere. We all know this fact. We were told this from the time we were very young, and we continue to tell it to our own children.

But do we actually live with this awareness? That is another question. The *yetzer harah* makes us think – sometimes even subconsciously – that we've fallen so far, that there is a great distance between us and our Creator. It seems like from such a low place, there is no way we can use our *avodas Hashem* to attach ourselves to Him.

Our davening is filled with such strange thoughts and foreign desires that we can't imagine that Hashem is *really* listening. We do our mitzvos by rote, with such little *kavanah*, as we don't really think that Hashem is paying attention to us. We know, in theory, that Hashem is everywhere; but, in practice, we couldn't feel further away from Him.

The foundation of Torah: No matter how low we fall, Hashem is still as close to us as ever.

Rebbe Nachman reveals to us that no matter how far we have fallen, and no matter how much we've forgotten about Hashem, He is still with us. He surrounds and fills the entire world, and there is no place that is void of His presence, like the verse says, "The whole world is filled with His glory (see Likutei Mohoran II 7:7)!" We may think that we've completely pushed Him out of our lives by refusing to listen to Him time after time, but He's still there. We may have given up on being close to Him, but He's still close to us and the warmth of His Presence is all around us.

Even if we find ourselves in the lowest places of darkness and despair, we have to believe that Hashem is still there. He is *mamash* living with us, watching every small thing that we do for Him lovingly and attentively. Our Sages say that the Shechinah rests above the head of the sick. If this is true about a physical sickness which only affects us in this world; it must certainly be true about a spiritual sickness which affects us in the next world as well.

The foundation of Torah and *avodas Hashem* is living with this *emunah*, as the verse says (*Tehillim* 119:86), "All of Your mitzvos are *emunah*!" In addition, our Sages say (Makos 24), "Chabakuk came and placed [the Torah] on one [principle] – a tzaddik lives with *emunah*."

With awareness of Hashem's Presence, we can awaken the fire of our *neshamah* and melt away the ice.

When we are a hundred percent certain that Hashem is really with us, then all the spiritual snow and ice that are covering our *neshamah* melt away, and our davening and mitzvos come alive. We realize that our *avodah* really matters and it is very important to Hashem. We're not just serving a king who we've never met before because he lives in some far away foreign country. Rather, we know that we are the King of all King's personal assistant. He gives us special orders – mitzvos – to carry out and He's grateful for everything that we do for Him.

When Hashem's Presence and constant Providence are real to us, then everything that we do to serve Him is full of inspiration. Every berachah we say becomes an opportunity to have a personal communicate with the Master of the Universe. Since we know that Hashem is listening to every word, our lifeless berachos are infused with *kavanah* and joy.

We no longer sin behind closed doors, and we find a true love for Hashem.

With this, we achieve fear of Heaven. We are so aware of Hashem's Presence that we feel we couldn't possibly sin before Him. We stop hiding behind closed doors as if no one sees us. Rather, the way that we act in public is exactly the same as the way we act in private. Even if we can't daven with a minyan in shul, we still try to pray slowly and say all of the words with *kavanah*.

In addition, we come to a deep love and awe of Hashem. We become aware of His greatness and glory which fill all of creation. When we daven *Pesukei d'Zimrah*, the verses of Dovid HaMelech that describe the wonders of creation inspire our heart and bring us to an amazement of Hashem. When we say the prayer of *Yotzer Ohr*, we shake in awe of the descriptions of the heavenly angels who serve the Almighty with such fiery brilliance. Now Hashem is so real to us, and all of His holy servants become real to us too.

When we say *Ahavah Rabbah*, we feel the deepest love that Hashem has for us. We feel just how incredibly special it is that He chose us to be His people and revealed His Torah to us. In turn, our hearts fill up with love for Hashem and we find a deep yearning to follow in His ways.

We become so attached to learning that it is hard for us to take a vacation.

Learning Torah stops being a burden that we are anxiously waiting to throw off our shoulders.

Rather, we constantly try to fill every single moment we can with Torah. *Bein hazmanim* and *bein hasedarim* cease to exist. There is no more need for summer vacation. We're so conscious of the unbelievable *nachas* that we give Hashem with every Mishnah, Gemorah, and Halachah that we learn; how could we possibly throw away such opportunities? Even when we're unable to sit for hours and go deep into a *sugyah*, we find true enjoyment by attaching ourselves to Hashem through learning the weekly parshah with Rashi.

Shabbos becomes a sweet taste of *Olam Habbah*.

With Hashem in our lives, we experience a true taste of the Next World on Shabbos. We feel the deep peacefulness in our mind and soul as the sun goes down and Shabbos comes in. We find the utmost *deveikus* in the tefillos of *Kabbalas Shabbos* and *Nishmas Kol Chai*. We relish the words of *Shemoneh Esrei* and say them slowly with sweetness and *kavanah*. When we realize that every moment that we're keeping Shabbos, we're revealing to the whole world the Oneness of Hashem's existence, our heart sings with joy all of the *zemiros* in the *bentcher*. We get up and dance with bliss in gratitude to Hashem for giving us Shabbos.

We treasure all of the specific mitzvos of each Yom Tov.

On Pesach, our matzah actually tastes like the sweetness of the manna, and our four cups of wine elevate us to complete *deveikus* in Hashem. We sing Hallel with all of our being and we feel the utmost closeness to the One who redeemed us from Egypt.

On Shavuos, it is not hard for us to stay awake the whole night, because we realize just how important our learning is to Hashem. When we go to the *mikveh* on Shavuos morning, we feel ourselves entering into the fiftieth gate of *kedushah* and being enveloped with Hashem's greatest compassion.

When the shofar blows on Rosh Hashanah, we feel our heart breaking with a deep desire to return to Hashem. On Yom Kippur, with each *vidui* we feel such an elevated sense of purity that even our hunger pangs can't distract us from serving Hashem.

On Succos, we can't put down our *daled minim*. We shake them and kiss them, knowing just how special they are to Hashem. When we sit in the succah, we are aware of the Shechinah resting in the *sechach* above our head. We enjoy being with Hashem in our succah so much that we have to force ourselves to leave when other obligations come up.

On Simchas Torah, we become so completely lost in the joy and delight that Hashem gave us the Torah that we dance and dance for hours without tiring.

When we light the Chanukah menorah, we feel Hashem's deepest compassion for us. With this mitzvah, Hashem has made it possible for us to bring the highest and most exalted light down into the darkest places of our lives. This comforts us and melts away all of our cold loneliness. Even the best party with the most delicious latkes and donuts, can't take us away from watching our candles until they finally burn out.

When we read the megillah on Purim, we see how Hashem has made miracles in our own personal lives and helped us to defeat our *yetzer harah* – also known as Haman (Amalek). With every sip of wine, we feel closer and closer to Him and we become filled with the true joy of being a Jew.

In short, by strengthening our faith that Hashem is *mamash* with us, the ice and snow feeling of being so far away from Him, simply dissolves with the warmth of His Presence. We find that our *neshamah* burns ever brighter with a deep yearning for Hashem. We find that our soul truly desires to serve Him with joy and inspiration. Our spiritual heart is beating, with a strong and alive fire for *avodas Hashem*.

> **True inspiration for *avodus Hashem* is not so far away; we just need to reignite the flame which is already inside us.**

This level of connection and inspiration might seem like something that's only for great tzaddikim, or perhaps the *ovdei Hashem* of previous generations. It might seem like serving Hashem with true love, awe, and *deveikus* are things that are simply beyond our reach. Maybe once when we were first starting out in *avodas Hashem* we tasted a little bit of this light, and we aspired to achieve it. But we failed so many times that we finally gave in to our *yetzer harah*, who convinced us that there's no hope for us to ever find that spark in our *avodah*.

However, we have to believe that this fire for Hashem is not so far away. It's not on the other side of the ocean and it's not all the way up in Heaven. Rather, we can attain it simply by strengthening our *emunah* that Hashem is still with us and as close to us as ever. The more that this *emunah* becomes clear to us, the more we begin to feel the warmth of our soul and its longing to be attached to its Source. Through this, we can find an amazing inspiration to serve Hashem.

Chizuk in Emunah

Chapter Six

The Illness: *My heart is so twisted with questions and doubts about Hashem and His ways.*

There is one word which causes many of us incredible suffering: *Why?* We go through our lives with our hearts and minds filled with continuous questions against Hashem: "Why me? Why is my life so hard? Why can't I make a decent living and afford all the things that my neighbors can afford? Why do I have to take care of such a sick child? Why do I have to deal with such an angry spouse? Why are my children going off the derech? It's just not fair. Why me?!

We are so accustomed to questioning Hashem that most of the time we don't even realize that we're doing it. It's just second nature. Because of this; we become very bitter about our lives, and sour in our behavior to other people.

Sometimes, when our lives become *so* difficult that we simply cannot handle it anymore; our questions go beyond our physical and emotional suffering and we may fall into serious doubts about the existence of Hashem, G-d forbid.

Countless Jews throughout history have stumbled down this path of destruction and become completely immersed in the secular world; may Hashem have compassion on their souls, and save us from such things.

The Rebbe's Prescription: Deep inside your heart there is a computer chip of faith that can help you fly over all of your questions and doubts. (Based on Likutei Moharan I, 64)

In the beginning, Hashem created an empty space that wasn't really empty.

For us to overcome all our questions and attach ourselves to Hashem with a full heart; we must *first* understand where our questions come from. We must *first* understand what is the spiritual source of all our *kashes* and doubts.

The *sefer Etz HaChaim* explains that before the Creation of the World, all that existed was the Eternal Light of Hashem. Since this light was perfect in its Oneness; there was no place for Hashem to create anything else: In a place of complete unity, it was not possible for Him to make distinct and differentiated worlds.

Therefore, Hashem moved the Light to both sides, so to speak, and made an empty space in the middle, void of all Light. Within this space that was distinct from the Eternal Light of Hashem; Hashem created all of the spiritual and physical Worlds. This is how all of existence came to be.

One big question arises from this teaching of the *Etz HaChaim*: The foundation of Judaism, as passed down from Avraham Avinu to all future generations, is the belief that there is only one G-d. Hashem is One and there is no other. He fills all the worlds and surrounds all the worlds, and there is no place which is vacant of His Presence. If so, how is it possible for an "empty space" to exist? How is it possible for there to be a place which is void of Hashem's Light?!

Based on this question, we're forced to say that Hashem's Light does exist even in the empty space. However, once we say that Hashem's Light really is in the empty space; then the empty space is no longer empty. If so, how could have Hashem created all the Worlds; since there is no place void of the Eternal Light of Hashem?

The more we try to tackle this question, the more we see that there is simply no answer. It is a complete contradiction which cannot be resolved according to human logic.

This inexplicable "empty space" is the source of our bitter questions about our lives.

It is because of this "empty space," that we fall into questions and difficulties with Hashem. In general, we believe that Hashem is One and there is no other. In fact, we proclaim this faith explicitly multiple times a day with the mitzvah of *Krias Shema*.

However, when things go wrong in our lives, we very easily fall into heretical beliefs as to the Oneness of Hashem. For example, we lose our job and we find ourselves deep in debt. Then, a family member gets really sick, G-d forbid. Not only are we now struggling to take care of them and the rest of our family; but we are no longer insured and the medical expenses are piling up. The result of this is that our marriage starts to suffer.

Next, our only car breaks down on the way to a crucial medical appointment. We find ourselves sitting on the side of the highway thinking, *"How is it possible for Hashem to exist in all of this? I'm suffering so much. I thought that Hashem was a compassionate G-d? Why do I have to go through this?!"* Because of all our questions, we lose our faith and fall far away from Hashem.

In order to find a way out of our questions and frustrations; we must first understand that all of our difficulties and suffering are coming from the "empty space." The teachings of Kabbalah and Chassidus explain this by saying that the empty space is the source of all *"din"* – judgement – in this World; since it is, so to speak, void the light of Hashem's compassion. It is from this place of *din*, that all seemingly "bad" things originate, and so, they are also apparently void of the compassion of Hashem.

In that empty space, we can't find Hashem or understand why we're suffering.

This is why we struggle so much – since we can't find Hashem in this empty space. If we were to see clearly that it was Hashem's Hand directly orchestrating our suffering; then we wouldn't have any questions at all. We would know that everything we're going through is for our best, since the Master of the Universe is showing that it is His Will. So, we would be able to accept our suffering with love and not get destroyed by it.

But, our suffering does not come from a place where Hashem is revealed. Rather, it comes from a place that is completely void of His Presence. Because of this; when we go through intense physical and spiritual suffering, we get filled with doubts about Hashem's existence. We fall into a place where we simply cannot find Him. No matter where we look, it seems as if He's not there.

There is a big black hole in the middle of Hashem's Oneness, and we get sucked into it. We grope around in the darkness, unable to see the Light of Hashem, and we slip into heretical thoughts, G-d forbid. Perhaps we still say *Krias Shema*, but we're not able to see the Oneness of Hashem in relation to what we're going through.

We know, in theory, that Hashem really is with us in our suffering. We know that Hashem is living with us in our "empty space," because if not, how could that space exist at all? Hashem's Presence fills all of the Worlds and surrounds all of the Worlds. Certainly, even in our most painful and desperate situations, Hashem has to be there.

However, we can't understand it at all. We can't understand why Hashem wants us to go through so many difficulties. We can't understand why we have to struggle so much to make a living. We can't understand why we have to have a family member with such a serious illness. We can't understand why we have to have such a difficult marriage. We can't understand how Hashem could be the One Who is causing us so much suffering. It doesn't make sense to us. The empty space that we're in seems to be really empty…

This is because the empty space from which our suffering comes, is a place that is completely beyond our understanding. On the one hand, it has to be empty; on the other hand, Hashem has to be there. The more we ask questions and try to understand this place; the more we fall deeper into doubt about Hashem's existence. In the empty space there are no answers, and the harder we look, the more difficulty we will have understanding the ways of Hashem.

The only way for us to attach to Hashem from this empty space is to connect to the root of our tradition: Emunah!

Therefore, we must attach ourselves to the essence of our soul that lies inside every single one of us. We must look deeply inside ourselves; beyond all of our physical, emotional, and psychological characteristics, and see who we truly are. What is a Jew? How could we describe our spiritual DNA? The answer is simple: A people of faith.

Avraham Avinu, as the first Jew, was called "the first of the believers." In a world of complete heresy and idol worship, Avraham put his entire life on the line to believe in One G-d. His father wanted to kill him and so did Nimrod, the most powerful man on earth. Nevertheless, Avraham wouldn't let go of his *emunah*. Hashem told him to leave his home and go to the land of Yisroel, and Avraham did so on pure faith.

When Avraham arrived there, all of a sudden there was a famine, and he was forced to go to Egypt. Avraham didn't question Hashem, and he went there with pure faith. Hashem told Avraham that he would have a son when he was a hundred years old and Sarah was ninety. Avraham believed Hashem with pure faith.

Then, after telling him that his descendants would be as great as the stars of the sky, Hashem told him to sacrifice his only son on an altar. Nevertheless, Avraham didn't question Hashem and followed Him with pure faith.

Avraham was the first to be called "Ivri" – Hebrew. Rebbe Nachman explains that this was because he was able to "pass over" all of these questions against Hashem. (The word "Ivri" in Hebrew has the same root as the word "Ohver," which means to pass over.) Through the unbelievable strength of his faith, Avraham was able to overcome all of his doubts about the Oneness of Hashem.

And it certainly didn't stop with Avraham. When we look at the lives of all the other six "shepherds of Yisroel" – Yitzchak, Yaakov, Yosef, Moshe, Aaron, and Dovid: We see that it was their incredible strength of faith that allowed them to come so close to Hashem, despite going through such incredible suffering.

The verse in *Tehillim* says (119:86), "All of Your mitzvos are *emunah!*" Additionally, our Sages say (Makos 24) that the prophet, Chabakuk, came and placed the entire Torah on one principle, "A tzaddik lives through his faith." From here, we see that *emunah* is the foundation of the Jewish tradition.

Hashem created the world in order for us to believe in His existence.

In fact, through *emunah* we can fulfill the entire purpose of Creation: to recognize Hashem's existence. Faith begins where understanding ends. Something that we can see with our own eyes or explain logically does not require any faith. It is *only* when we encounter something which is entirely beyond our understanding that we must have faith.

Therefore, as finite creatures, our greatest accomplishment in this world is to believe with our entire heart in that which is beyond our understanding: the existence of the Infinite. This is why Hashem created us. This is why we have to suffer and go through the "empty space" which is void of all understanding. It is all in order to bring us to recognize the Oneness of Hashem through our faith.

This faith is our greatest inheritance from our ancestors and it is what keeps us alive today. Indeed, how is it that the Jews have survived such a long and bitter exile since the destruction of the second Temple almost two thousand years ago? After all the immense suffering that we've gone through, it is very difficult to understand how we're still here. What is the difference between us and all the other nations of the past which no longer exist? The answer is once again very simple: our *emunah* in Hashem!

Through finding this spark of *emunah* within us, we can fly over all of our suffering.

Therefore, even if we sometimes feel completely distant from this belief – that everything that happens to us comes only from Hashem – we know that deep inside of our being, there is a spark of pure faith. It has to exist! Without it, we wouldn't be here at all.

Although we have doubts and questions, at the end of the day we know that we have *neshamah* – a piece Hashem Himself – within us. Therefore, we must remember that the essence of that *neshamah* is *emunah*. This is who we are at our core, and through this we can rise above all of our questions.

By attaching ourselves to our faith, we can fly over and escape the "empty space" of our suffering. There is no way for us to understand what's happening to us, but we don't need to. We have amazing wings that can carry us over all of our pain. We have wings which can lift us above all of our problems. We don't need to know why we're going through what we're going through; since we know and believe that Hashem is with us in the darkness. Everything is completely for our best. There is nothing but Hashem… completely nothing but Hashem!

Through our faith, we can see that everything that happens to us is Divine Providence. Through our faith, we can find the strength to endure even the most difficult challenges with a smile on our face. Through our faith, we can connect to Hashem even from our empty space.

When our faith is asleep, we must use our speech to bring it back to life (see Likutei Mohoran II, 44).

However, for many of us our faith lies dormant inside of us. It has been in hibernation for years, even decades, and maybe, for even our entire life. We desperately want to cling to Hashem even in the most difficult situations; but when push comes to shove, it feels as if our *emunah* is asleep, and we don't know how to wake it up.

In such situations, Rebbe Nachman says that the tool for bringing it back to life is by simply expressing our *emunah* out loud. Even if we feel in our hearts that our faith is very weak and frail; nevertheless, we should say out loud, "*Hashem, I know You're with me. I know that You are One, and everything that I'm going through is only for the best.*" Even if our minds are filled with questions about Hashem; we must force ourselves to repeat over and over "*Ein oid milvado* – there is nothing other than Hashem!"

Even though we may feel like we're lying, we must pretend like we really believe and express our *emunah* in words: "Hashem, I can't understand why I have to suffer, but I know that You have a reason. It could be an atonement for my sins. It could be a tikkun for a previous incarnation (gilgul). It could be, simply, in order to give me greater reward in the Next World. Whatever it is, I believe that nothing that's happening to me is stam, and it's all completely good. Gam zu letova!"

Through speaking out our faith, we slowly but surely increase our level of *emunah*. Speech has an incredible power of transformation. If we simply say something over and over again, we begin to believe that this is *actually* true. For example, if we tell ourselves that we are a certain way and we have certain characteristics; in time, we will develop those characteristics. If we constantly tell ourselves that we are bad people and we *always* mess up; then this becomes a self-fulfilling prophecy and we will continuously make mistakes. On the other hand, if we say constantly that we are really good Jews and that we believe strongly in Hashem; then we will, eventually, develop a deep level of faith.

Prayer is a pure expression of *emunah*.

In addition to speaking out our faith, we can also turn to Hashem in prayer and ask for His help. Even if we're extremely far from living with *emunah*, we can express to Hashem our deepest yearning to have real faith. We can ask Hashem, "Please help me to have the faith to endure and overcome everything that I'm going through. Please strengthen me to believe that You are *mamash* here, even in this 'empty space' of my life."

Through prayer, not only do we receive Divine assistance; rather the process of davening itself also strengthens our *emunah*. Tefillah is an expression of faith. By turning to Hashem for help, we show Hashem, and more importantly ourselves, just how deeply we believe in His ability to save us. It is really a very simple equation: the more we daven, the stronger our faith.

There is no other *avodah* that will nurture our *emunah* more than tefillah. We could learn Torah without actually connecting it to Hashem, G-d forbid. We could even do mitzvos by rote, without thinking about Hashem at all. But when we plead with Him to give us true *emunah*; we strengthen our faith that the Master of the Universe exists in our life.

Ideally, our prescribed daily prayers should build our *emunah* as well. However, since so many of us are accustomed to saying these prayers on a regular basis; many of us end up reciting them without thinking about Hashem at all. Therefore, the best remedy is personal prayer. By expressing our faith in our own words, we nurture within ourselves a real connection to our Source. When we establish an authentic relationship with our Creator – not only does this bond strengthen our ability to relate to Hashem in our prescribed prayers – it also brings Hashem into all aspects of our life, even when we're lost in the abyss in the "empty space" of our suffering.

Through this, we can awaken that computer chip of faith which was given to us by our holy ancestors. Through this, we can begin to live with true *emunah* on a day-to-day basis. Through this, we can fly like a bird over all of our questions and doubts. We can free ourselves from all of our questions. We can find inner peace and calmness amidst the storm.

By awakening our faith, we find true happiness.

Once we reach this place of faith, a wondrous thing happens: we become happy! When we know that everything is for the best, no matter what we're going through, then we are filled with joy. We're able to lift ourselves out of our depression and anger which are caused by our questions, and find true contentment. Nothing could be better in our life. We're happy with our physical and spiritual lot in This World. Everything is completely good. It's amazing!

We no longer get bothered by every little thing that doesn't go our way. We no longer get upset with life's challenges. Rather, these things don't affect us, and even more, they can't knock us down into total darkness. When we live with the faith that – even though, it seems like we're surrounded by the complete chaos of the "empty space" – everything is really coming from the holy Eternal Light of Hashem, then there is nothing else to do but rejoice!

We begin to sing a song of *deveikus* to Hashem.

This joy inspires us to sing a niggun. In fact, our entire life becomes an extraordinary melody. In general, we begin to listen to and sing a lot of music; but it's not necessarily the music that inspires us to *avodas Hashem*. It may make us feel good in a physical way, but it doesn't make our soul happy. It doesn't have the ability to get us out of our depression. On the contrary, most modern music (even what's considered "Jewish music") usually increases our physical desires and makes us sink deeper into sadness.

This is because the spiritual source of this music is the brokenness and darkness of the "empty space." The music that comes from "such a place" will only increase our suffering and make us feel further away from Hashem.

With a strengthened *emunah*, however; we start yearning for the niggun which will inspire our *neshamah* to serve Hashem. We start longing to sing a holy song of faith, through which we can attach ourselves to Hashem with complete joy and deveikus.

We begin singing our davening with an exquisite melody, which we improvise each day. We begin to sing every berachah and every word of Torah out loud, with a joyous tune. We listen to the songs of the tzaddikim, whose unbelievable *emunah* has carried them through all the difficulties of the exile. These songs of our tzaddikim are so deeply rooted in the truest faith that they can be incredible channels for us to rise above the questions of the "empty space" and reconnect with the Eternal Light of Hashem, which is hidden there.

These songs of faith and inspiration have such a sweetness that they can nullify all of our doubts and questions. When we taste the pure connection to Hashem through the song of *emunah*, we no longer need an answer to our *kashes*. Our whole entire being is enveloped with the joy and clarity of experiencing Hashem's Oneness.

Through our song of faith, we come to a clearer awareness of Hashem and taste the consciousness of redemption (see Likutei Mohoran I, 7).

The result of our happiness is that we achieve *yishuv hadaas*. Through our song of faith and joy, we're able to liberate our minds from its inner cloud of darkness. We're able to get our thoughts out of a state of exile, and come to a truer awareness of Hashem. When we are sad, our mind is confused and constricted. We feel too tired to think about anything; let alone put our head into a Gemara or try to daven with *kavanah*.

However, through the joy of our *emunah*, we're able to free our mind from all of its huge tangle of cobwebs. We're able to break free of our many worries and fears that weigh us down, and experience an aspect of the sweetness of expanded consciousness (*mochin de'gadlus*) of the times of Mashiach, as the verse says (Yishaya 55), "Through happiness, you will go out [of exile]."

Even though we must always yearn and pray for the ultimate Redemption of the Jewish people – *may it come speedily and in our days, amen!* – nevertheless, we have the ability right now to escape our own internal exile. Instead of waiting helplessly for Mashiach to come and save us, we can live in "Mashiach-consciousness" right now.

Our Sages say (Nedarim 41), "If you acquire *daas*, what are you lacking? If you're lacking *daas*, what have you acquired?" The *"daas"* that the Sages refer to cannot be translated as "knowledge," since it is clear that someone could know a lot of Torah, but without *emunah*, he could still feel deeply lacking in his life. Rather, the word *"daas"* in this case means "awareness of Hashem," which we achieve through faith, as explained above.

So, we see from the wisdom of our Sages that the ultimate perfection that we are striving for is the constant awareness of Hashem's Presence. When we have this *"daas,"* we don't feel like we're missing anything in our life at all. It could seem on the outside like everything is going completely wrong – we have no money, we're in bad health, our children don't listen to anything we say – but in our minds' eye everything is fine; since we know that what we're going through is exactly what Hashem wants for us. It is exactly what we need to reach our ultimate goal.

This awareness is what Mashiach will bring to mankind, as the verse says (Yishaya 11), "And the world will be filled with the awareness (*daas*) of Hashem, like the waters which cover the sea."

Additionally, by strengthening our faith, we can be proactive in bringing Mashiach. Our Sages say (Sotah 3) that a person *only* sins when he isn't in his right mind. So, when we're able to clear our heads and awaken a constant awareness of Hashem through the joy of *emunah*; then we can do a complete teshuvah and refrain from *all* transgressions.

The Sages also say (Yuma 86) that the Final Redemption is dependent only on teshuvah. Therefore, by freeing our thoughts from their exile and returning to Hashem; we can do our part to bring the collective Redemption as well. This is what is in our hands right now, at this moment.

Faith is the difference between life and death, exile and redemption.

To conclude, we must know that we *can* make the choice between life and death. Without *emunah*, our life is full of suffering. We can't understand why everything is always going wrong. We have no way to comfort ourselves. We are lost in an empty space, void of the Light of Hashem. We fall into a state of exile and brokenness, filled with anger and frustration (see Sichos HaRan, 32).

However, through *emunah* we can live a good life. No matter what happens to us, we know Hashem is with us. Through our faith, we can comfort ourselves in our suffering; since we know that we're not alone. Even though we can't understand it, we know that the "empty space" is really filled with Hashem's Light and love. We have a way to escape our pain, by attaching ourselves evermore strongly to Hashem with *emunah*. Through this, we can be happy and serve Hashem with all our heart and soul.

The verse says (Shir HaShirim 4), "Come [out of exile] and sing, through the highest faith." From here, we see the power of the song of faith and joy. Through this song, we can find true awareness of Hashem. Through this song, we can merit to see the coming of Mashiach, speedily and in our days, amen!

Chapter Seven

The Illness: It feels like I have to work very hard to do mitzvos, and I'm always falling short.

For many of us, *avodas Hashem* feels like a huge mountain which is very difficult to climb. We learn all the halachos pertaining to a certain mitzvah; but then when it comes to performing that mitzvah, we struggle greatly to carry it out with all of its correct details.

Additionally, even when we manage to climb the mountain and do a mitzvah; we often fall into doubt if we really fulfilled our obligation or not... Perhaps, the way that we did the mitzvah was slightly incorrect and the small error we made caused the entire mitzvah to be disqualified... This causes us to be very nervous when we perform mitzvos and makes it impossible for us to connect to Hashem and feel inspired in our *avodah*.

The Rebbe's Prescription: By strengthening your faith in yourself, serving Hashem becomes easy and enjoyable. (Based on Likutei Mohoran II, 86 and Likutei Halachos, Pikadon 5:7)

> **We must believe in our capability to give Hashem *nachas* through our mitzvos, despite their imperfections.**

In order to find inspiration and joy in our *avodas Hashem*, we must acquire three aspects of faith. Firstly, we must believe that Hashem exists. We must believe that there is One G-d who created the Heavens and the Earth, and chose to give His Torah and mitzvos to the Jewish people. This is a given.

The second aspect is that we must have faith in the Prophets, Sages and tzaddikim of all time, who have carried the oral tradition all the way from Har Sinai until today. Without them, we wouldn't have any idea how to perform the mitzvos which are written in the Torah. It is only through their teachings that we know what is Hashem's will. For any religious Jew, this aspect is also a given.

However, there is a third aspect of faith that many of us struggle with, which is equally important and integral to our connection to *avodas Hashem*: we must believe in ourselves! We must believe that even if we fall to the lowest spiritual depths; we still have the ability to serve Hashem and give Him *nachas*. We must believe that whatever we're able to do for Hashem – even if it is full of mistakes and far from perfect – is a priceless treasure in His eyes.

This third aspect of *emunah* is absolutely crucial. No matter how strongly we believe in Hashem and our tzaddikim; when we lack faith in ourselves, *avodas Hashem* feels very difficult and burdensome. It seems like we're unable to do anything to please the Almighty. We try our hardest to do mitzvos on a level of perfection beyond our capability, and we constantly fall short. This causes us great frustration and turns our mitzvos into lifeless vessels, void of any inspiration.

Hashem is not expecting us to be angels!

Indeed, we must remember what our Sages teach us (*Kiddushin* 54), "The Torah was not given to the ministering angels!" Hashem is not expecting us to be perfect. He's *not* expecting us to perform each mitzvah, with all of its stringencies (see Likutei Mohoran II, 44).

Hashem loves us just the way that we are, with all of our blemishes and imperfections. He loves every single attempt that we make to serve Him, even if we can't do mitzvos in their ideal fashion. Our "*bedieved*" is precious gold to Hashem. In fact, if we made a true effort to do a mitzvah, even though we didn't fulfill our obligation at all; nevertheless, Hashem treasures our effort and considers it as if we succeeded.

Our Sages also say (*Avodah Zarah 3a*) that Hashem doesn't come with a plot against His Creations. This means that Hashem knows the strength of our *yetzer harah* and He understands how much we are struggling to overcome it. In light of this, He doesn't expect us to do more than we can in any given moment. If we sincerely try to do our best, He doesn't judge us for not fulfilling all of the details of a particular mitzvah.

We see from here that Hashem believes in us. He believes in our ability to rectify the entire world, even if we can't serve Him like the true tzaddikim. If so, we should also believe in our ability to serve Hashem and we shouldn't have lofty, unrealistic expectations. We should see that by simply trying to keep the basic halachah, we are sustaining the entire universe!

When we finish a mitzvah, we should be confident that it was received in Heaven.

With this knowledge, we will come to realize that there's no reason for us to have doubts about a mitzvah after we've finished it. Most of the time, the uncertainty we have is just a product of our fear of failure. We're worried that, perhaps, what we did was not good enough and we must try to reach a higher level of perfection.

However, there is nothing to be afraid of! In Hashem's eyes, our mitzvah is the most precious jewel. Even if we didn't meet the requirements; nevertheless, we don't need to dwell on our doubts and insecurities. Rather, we can be confident that what we did was good enough, knowing that it's okay to be imperfect in our *avodah*.

(Note: This obviously excludes cases where it seems very likely that we didn't fulfill our basic obligation, and we still have an opportunity to fix or redo it again. In such cases, we should follow the halachah and make another attempt.)

Chumros are often an incredibly mischievous disguise for our *yetzer harah*.

Additionally, not only are extra stringencies not necessary in order to give Hashem *nachas*; they are often very harmful to our *avodas Hashem*. Even though we may have very good, altruistic intentions for keeping them, these *chumros* can actually be a clever disguise for our *yetzer harah*.

Since every single mitzvah we do is fulfilling the purpose of all Creation, our *yetzer harah* does whatever he can to stop us. One of his most common tactics is trying to convince us to do too much. He tells us that in order to do the mitzvah properly, we must first climb a mountain of *chumros*. His argument is very convincing, since after all, *chumros* are stated in the books of halachah.

So, we fall for his trick and begin climbing… Most of us, however, don't have the spiritual strength to make it to the top of the mountain. So, after a while, we fall to the bottom and give up on doing that mitzvah altogether. Or perhaps, we are so overwhelmed that we never even start climbing at all. And so the *yetzer harah* wins.

However, little do we know that we can accomplish the mitzvah without having to work so hard. We don't have to make it all the way to the top of the mountain. Rather, if we just make it a little way up, we've already arrived! Simply by following basic halachah to the best of our ability, we've achieved an incredible feat.

With this perspective, serving Hashem becomes easy and enjoyable. We don't need to push ourselves beyond our capabilities. Instead, we can do each mitzvah with whatever strength we have at that moment, and easily fulfill Hashem's will. Through this, we can also enjoy the process of doing mitzvos and serving Hashem.

It was her stringencies that caused Chava to sin.

In fact, the mistake of being too strict goes all the way back to the sin of Chava in Gan Eden. When the snake asked her if any tree was forbidden; she replied that Hashem had forbidden them from touching the Tree of Knowledge, when in fact the prohibition was *only* not to eat from it. The snake then pushed her into the tree, showing her that there was no punishment for touching it. After that, he convinced her that just like there was no punishment for touching the tree; so too, it was okay to eat from its fruit. With this, Chava transgressed Hashem's word and committed the most grievous sin of all time (see Rashi on Bereishis 3:3).

From here, we see that we must be careful not to be too stringent. We must try not to do too much. Rather, we must focus on the incredible value of the basic halachah, and not expect to achieve perfection.

The verse says (Devarim 30:12), "*Lo bashamayim hi ... ve'lo me'ever hayam* – the Torah is not in Heaven and it's not on the other side of the sea!" Rather, it's very close to us. It's in our hands and ability to do it. We don't need to be stringent in our observance of mitzvos in order to please Hashem and fulfill our purpose in This World.

By following the basic halachah without extra *chumros*; it is much easier to perform Hashem's mitzvos with love and awe.

Not only is this true for those of us who not are able to be extremely stringent with our mitzvos; rather, the same is true even for those who *are* capable of carrying out mitzvos with all of their *chumros*. The reason is that when we try to be exceedingly *machmir* while doing a mitzvah, we focus so much on our precision, that we end up performing the mitzvah in a very robotic way. It is as if we're simply pressing buttons to command our limbs to move a certain way to get the mitzvah done.

With this, we totally squash any potential to truly connect to Hashem while serving Him. In fact, often we're *so* preoccupied with our *chumros*, that we can't even think about Hashem at all while we're doing the mitzvah.

Therefore, if we find ourselves trying to be very *machmir*, we should ask ourselves: *Is this really how Hashem wants us to serve Him? No!* Our Sages say, "The Compassionate One wants our heart!" He wants us serve Him with love and awe. He wants us to do His mitzvos with the utmost *deveikus* and joy!

Take, for example, the mitzvah of *Krias Shema*. It is stated in halachah numerous details as to how we must pronounce the words of the Shema. Some of these halachos are essential to fulfilling our obligation, while many others are extra stringencies. For most of us, if we were to try to say the Shema with every single *chumrah*, it would come out as an extremely mechanical recitation.

Even when we say the words, "And you shall love Hashem, your G-d, with all of your heart, and all of your soul, and all of your means," we wouldn't be able to feel any connection to the Almighty. We might be so busy with our *chumros*, that we could even forget that the entire purpose of the mitzvah is to receive upon ourselves the Kingship of Heaven and give our entire life over to Hashem, with pure faith in His absolute Oneness. Additionally, we might be so nervous and shaky because of our stringencies that we have a really hard time just getting the words out at all.

However, by keeping the basic halachah and not concerning ourselves with the extra *chumros*, we have the capability to say *Krias Shema* from our heart with joy and attachment to our Creator. We're not just fulfilling our obligation by reciting a passage from the Torah; rather we're living it and experiencing it! We are aware of Hashem's Presence as we do the mitzvah and we feel the incredible *nachas* that we're giving Him, with every single word.

Of course, it goes without saying that if we're able to experience deep love and awe of Hashem; while at the same time being precise and fulfilling all of the stringencies, then all the more is this pleasing to Hashem. There is no need to erase the *chumros* from the books of halachah, G-d forbid, since there are select individuals, even in the extraordinary darkness of this generation, who are able to carry out all of the details without sacrificing in their *deveikus* to Hashem.

Rather, the point is that today most of us are too lost in our physical desires and lack true *yishuv hadaas*, We should recognize this and not try to do too much. We must believe in ourselves that—despite our inability to serve Hashem with perfection – we can still do great things. Simply by following basic halachah, we are purifying our souls of darkness and contamination. When we strengthen this faith further, we find a deepened inspiration to serve Hashem and attach ourselves to His mitzvos with joy. This, in turn, makes our mitzvos even more powerful tools of rectification.

Being too *machmir* takes precious time away from other important aspects of *avodas Hashem* (see Sichos HaRan, 30).

Additionally, there is another downside to being too strict in our practice of mitzvos: we sacrifice precious time which could be used for learning and davening. The *halachic sefarim* mention certain categories that we are obliged to search and clean, while others are only extra stringencies.

Many of us take it upon ourselves to follow all the *chumros*, which causes us to spend an exorbitant amount of time cleaning. We use countless extra hours and days to fulfill all of the stringencies, and we leave ourselves very little time to learn, daven, and do all the other important daily mitzvos in the Torah.

On the other hand, by simply keeping the basic halachah; we will have more time to dedicate to other aspects of *avodas Hashem*. We don't have to sacrifice our performance in other areas of the Torah, in order to ensure that our home is perfectly clean of *chametz*. Rather, we're able to achieve all the requirements of the mitzvah of *bedikas chametz*, and spend hours a day in the *beis midrash*.

It is good to have one mitzvah as our specialty.

In spite of all that has been said, Rebbe Nachman does recommend that we chose one mitzvah in which we keep all of the chumros (see Sichos HaRan, 235). Thus, we should find a mitzvah that we have a natural talent for and we really love to do. For this one mitzvah alone; we should try our best to go beyond the letter of the law and fulfill its stringencies.

However, even with this mitzvah we must be careful not to take it too far and become too obsessive. Instead, even while trying to do the mitzvah with its *chumros*, we should remember that even without the *chumros*, our mitzvah gives Hashem unbelievable *nachas*. So, at the same time that we're aiming for perfection; we're also aware that whatever the result may be, we will be pleased with it. With this, we are able to keep our emotional connection to the mitzvah and our attachment to Hashem.

Each one of our mitzvos is an eternal merit.

To conclude, in the process of doing mitzvos we must believe that whatever we are capable of at any given moment is more than enough. Our *avodas Hashem* is able to transform and rectify all the Worlds just the way it is, with all of its imperfections.

Therefore, even if we fail to fulfill the mitzvah as we hoped, or perhaps we didn't even meet the basic criteria; we should *still* be overjoyed with our attempt. Even just our efforts to do mitzvos gives great splendor to Hashem; all the more so if we're able to fulfill its main requirements.

After we've completed a mitzvah, we shouldn't have any doubts about whether it was good enough or not. Rather, we should believe with all our hearts that we certainly did a great deed which will never be erased, and will remain a merit for all eternity.

Chapter Eight

The Illness: It seems like everything in my life is going wrong and I never get a break.

Sometimes, it appears to us like nothing ever goes our way. We feel like life is one long and bitter process of suffering. We never have the money that we need, and we fall deep into debt. We look for a better-paying job, but somehow we never manage to get one. Then, our boss says that he's letting us go; he says that we do good work, but the company is downsizing. He is ever so sorry!

Then, one of our kids gets really sick, G-d forbid. So, we have to schlep him around from doctor to doctor to try to help him. The problem is that we are no longer insured, so the medical bills start piling up.

With all the stress at home, our marriage starts to fall apart. It feels like we're constantly at war with our spouse over every little thing. We can't even stand being at home.

It seems like things can't get any worse. Our life is only pain and suffering and we lose all hope for the future. We think that this is it, and there simply is no way out…

The Rebbe's Prescription: Even the midst of the worst suffering, you can find moments of relief and glimmers of hope that will carry you to salvation. (Based on Likutei Mohoran I, 185)

> **Even though we can't understand Hashem's ways; we must believe that everything He does is completely good.**

It is human nature to want to live a good life. We want our family to be healthy. We want to get a lot of *yiddishe nachas* from our children. We want to make a good living in order to acquire the possessions we need.

Of course, Hashem also wants us to have everything good in our lives. He wants to take care of every single one of our needs. He wants to open up the Heavens and rain down all of His blessings upon us. He wants to give us His bounty not only in the next world, rather even in this world as well.

However, the reality is that in order for us to do teshuvah, or in order to purify us of our sins from this incarnation or a previous one, or for a number of other reasons which we cannot understand, Hashem doesn't allow our lives to go so smoothly. Perhaps, the only way for us to come to recognize Him and attach ourselves to Him is that we must be poor and have to daven constantly for His assistance. Perhaps, the only way to atone for certain sins that we've committed is that we have to go through physical suffering, G-d forbid. Whatever the reason is we can never know; but for sure there is a reason!

During tough times when it is very difficult, we can't question Hashem's ways; we have to believe that somehow everything is for the best. We have to believe that what we're going through is a hundred percent Divine Providence in order to help us get closer to Him in some way. The main purpose of our existence on this earth is to grow and deepen our faith in Hashem.

Our happiness and suffering are dependent on the level of our faith.

The more that we strengthen this belief, the more we're able to escape our suffering; since we're able to understand that everything that's happening to us is completely good. The clearer our *emunah* in the pure loving-kindness of Hashem; the more we will be able to find true happiness in this world, no matter what we're going through. So, we must continually strive to strengthen our faith and receive whatever Hashem gives us with love.

However, for most of us whose *emunah* is not so strong; especially when we're really being tested, it feels like it is nearly impossible for us to find comfort. At the end of the day, we *still* feel the sickness in our body, and we *still* feel hopeless when we look at our enormous credit card bills. We may know and even try to remind ourselves that everything is for the best and, somehow, Hashem will help; but it is so hard to really "live" with this reality, so we continue to suffer without any respite or relief. We remain bitter towards Hashem and give up on serving Him, G-d forbid. We wait for the day that Mashiach will knock on the door with a million dollars and medicines for all of our illnesses, but the days pass and we're still waiting…

By finding relief amidst his troubles, Dovid HaMelech was able to constantly praise Hashem.

Therefore, until Mashiach comes to bring us complete relief from all of our suffering – speedily and in our days, *amen!* – Rebbe Nachman gives us a way to repair and strengthen our faith in order to find hope and contentment with our lives. He explains that, although it may seem to us like everything that happens to us is bad without exception and our lives are one long thread of pain and despair; this is not really true. Even in the most difficult situations, it is possible to find moments of respite and glimmers of hope.

The best example of this is from Dovid HaMelech, may he rest in peace. Dovid HaMelech suffered perhaps more than any other person in the history of time. He was a complete reject in his family, and considered by all an illegitimate child. Shaul Hamelech himself chased him down and tried to kill him. Throughout his life, he was threatened to death, even by his own son, Avshalom. His existence was constantly hanging on a hairsbreadth. If we were to examine all of his trials and tribulations, we would certainly find that he had absolutely no reason to be happy and praise Hashem.

And yet, it was Dovid Hamelech who composed *sefer Tehillim*, the greatest book of praise and thanks to Hashem in all of history! *How did he do it?* The answer is that even in the most impossibly difficult situations, he was able to find and focus on aspects of respite and relief, and give thanks to Hashem.

For example, the verse in *Tehillim* says (Chapter 4), "In the midst of my suffering, You gave me relief." It doesn't say that You "removed my suffering." Rather, even though things were still not going well and he was surrounded by darkness on all sides, Dovid was able to find Hashem's relief.

Our Sages show (Brachos 7a) another example of this from *sefer Tehillim*. The verse says, "A song for Dovid, as he fled from Avshalom, his son." Our Sages ask, how could Dovid Hamelech sing a song about how he was chased by his own son who was trying to kill him? "A lamentation for Dovid," would have been more appropriate. Our Sages answer that since it was Dovid's own son who was chasing him; Dovid knew that Avshalom would have more compassion on him than any other person who was seeking his life.

This is a constant theme throughout the entire *sefer Tehillim*.

We too, must see the unbelievable *yeshuos* all around us!

From the life of Dovid HaMelech, we can also find a way to strengthen our faith, and be hopeful and even happy in the midst of our suffering.

Although it may seem to us like we have no money and that we are deep in debt; we must remember that we're not living in a cardboard box in Bombay with torrential monsoon rains pouring down on top of us. Thank G-d, we have a roof over our head! Even though our apartment may feel much too small and cramped for our large family, nevertheless, we have a home. We're not sleeping on the streets!

Although we can't pay off our entire debt at once, we should see that every time we are able to pay off a little bit is an incredible *yeshuah* from Hashem. Instead of not being satisfied with our job as it's not paying the bills; we should thank Hashem that we're making some money and we're not unemployed. Every time we make a berachah and eat some food, we should recognize the amazing miracle Hashem performed for us to be able to survive. Thank G-d; we and our children are not starving to death in Africa.

We should do the same when it comes to our health. Even though our family may be suffering from a flu which is getting passed around from one member to the next; we can find relief that at least we're not all sick at the same time and the healthy ones are there to take care of the sick. And even if our whole family is sick, we can find relief in that it's not a serious illness and it will soon pass.

But, even if we or one of our children or parents are suffering from a terminal illness, G-d forbid, we can thank Hashem for every moment that we're alive. Although we may not have so much strength to daven and serve Hashem, we can find respite in each word of *tefillah* and every mitzvah that we're still able to do. Because of our physical suffering, we should see that every little thing we do in *avodas Hashem* is so much more precious to Him

And even if we lose a family member, G-d forbid and may we all live to 120, we can find relief that at least we have faith in the Next World; where we know that they will live for eternity in the light of Hashem.

In addition, we must look at our children with the same perspective. Although our young children seem like they're constantly complaining, whining, and screaming in our ears to the point of insanity; we must see that there are moments of peace and quiet. There are *even* times when our children act respectfully towards us and say, "Thank you!" Even though it may be incredibly difficult to raise them, we should be grateful to Hashem for every time they say a berachah, put on tzitzis or a *kippah*, or learn one Mishnah.

Even if our children are not doing well in yeshivah or seminary, we can find respite in the fact that they're still keeping Shabbos and following halachah. And even if, G-d forbid, they leave the Torah completely; we can still find relief that they are Jews, and in some way they are still giving *nachas* to Hashem, like our Sages say, "Even the sinners of Yisroel are full of mitzvos like a pomegranate." Maybe they still wear a *kippah*, no matter what color, shape, or size it may be. Perhaps, they still don't eat shrimp or bacon. Even though these things seem completely insignificant in relation to all of their transgressions; we must believe that they are incredibly important to Hashem.

The greatest relief is the simple fact that we follow Hashem's Torah.

At the end of the day, no matter what is happening to us and no matter what insanely difficult challenges we're going through; we can always find relief in the fact that we are *frum* Jews. In today's day and age, in which the infectious disease of atheism has almost completely devoured the entire world – non-Jews and Jews alike – we merit to be the last few who are hanging on to their faith. Amazing!

In a world more greedy for money than any other idol worship in all of history; we have the merit of keeping Shabbos where we break away from our obsession for wealth. Even if we feel like we're always chasing the god of money; at least for one day a week we don't go to work, our phone is off, and we recognize the Creator of the universe. Unbelievable!

In a world where most people recite the disgusting lyrics to rap and pop songs; we are reciting the unbelievably holy *lashon* of the *Shemoneh Esrei* three times a day. We say berachos over everything we put into our mouth. We say *Krias Shema* and unify Hashem's name. We proclaim, "Blessed are You Who spoke and the world came into existence!" Incredible!

In a world where people eat the most despicable creatures and dress in the most immodest clothing; we sanctify our bodies with kosher food and respectful attire. In a world where marriage has nearly ceased to exist and gender is a matter of opinion; we keep the holy laws purity in our homes and do our best to raise children. *Unfathomable!*

These are real *yeshuos*. No matter what we're going through both physically and spiritually, if we focus on these things and thank Hashem for each and every one of them; we will find true relief from all of our suffering.

Through this, we can strengthen our faith and open our heart in prayer.

The result of this is truly astonishing. We find the courage to hope and believe that Hashem is good. We see that, even though things are very hard, there are sparks of salvation all around us. We don't feel like our life is completely bad and Hashem doesn't care, G-d forbid. Rather, we recognize that Hashem really is helping us.

This greatly strengthens our *emunah* in all of the things that we simply cannot understand. When we see before our eyes the miracles that Hashem has done for us, day in and day out, then we can let go of all of our questions and problems, and simply believe in Him. We can close our eyes from the apparent darkness which surrounds us and have faith in the light that is hidden inside of it. There is nothing but Hashem! He is completely One, and His Oneness is completely good!

This faith gives us the strength to daven. We realize that, although it may seem nearly impossible, Hashem can save us. Even though things may be very, very dark, we mustn't fall into complete despair. Rather, we should open our hearts to Hashem in prayer and pour out our deepest desire to escape our physical and spiritual suffering.

We should beg Hashem to help us pay off all our debts and to be able to support our family. We must plead with Hashem over and over again to bring our children home from the distant places they have strayed. We must daven to Hashem to heal us from our sicknesses and give us the strength to serve Him.

When we say these prayers from a place of gratitude for Hashem's constant kindness and hope for our ultimate salvation, they have unbelievable spiritual power. When we daven with a pure belief in Hashem's ability to help us, then nothing can stop our tefillos from reaching His Throne of Glory (see Likutei Halachos, Kilei Behema 4).

By strengthening our faith, we rekindle our relationship with Hashem and create a new channel for Him to bestow upon us all of His blessings. We begin to see our prayers being answered and this strengthens us even more in our davening. Even though in the past, it seemed to us that there was no way that *tefillah* would ever help us; now with renewed faith, we begin to see that *tefillah* really works!

The small *yeshuos* start coming more and more frequently, and we even find bigger ones coming in from all sides. Perhaps, after a while, we're able to completely pay off our credit cards. Perhaps, we witness a family member completely recover from a terminal illness and see the hand of Hashem clearly in our lives.

Although we may never see a complete salvation from all of our problems, that is simply the nature of this world. We're not here for vacation. We're here to rectify our souls and all of Hashem's Creation. Until Mashiach comes, it's never going to be just a walk in the park.

However, through the practice of finding respite amidst our suffering; we're no longer just trying to survive this world and all of its bitterness. We're no longer in such despair that we can hardly serve Hashem. We're no longer trying to run away from the burden of our responsibilities.

Rather, with these moments of relief and respite, we're able to be happy with every little bit of good that we have and are hopeful to Hashem for the future. We're able to strengthen our faith and live with Hashem throughout our suffering. Since we know that Hashem really cares about us and is taking care of us; we're able to escape our worries and fears, and open our heart to Him in prayer.

We're able to find a deep strength and patience to endure life's greatest challenges. Even when everything around us seems like it's falling apart, we're not falling. Instead, we're praising Hashem for every moment of relief and spark of hope, and attaching ourselves to Him with true hope and joy.

Chizuk in Simchah

Chapter Nine

The Illness: I feel so depressed and lazy, and I have no strength for avodas Hashem.

Depression is a sickness that has taken over the world. It has infected both men and women of all ages and spread to all nations and cultures, quickly sucking the life out of the human race.

When we fall into depression, it is as if there is a dark storm cloud covering our head which is extracting every ounce of energy from our brain and our body. We can't learn Torah because our mind is like mush. It's hard for us to even walk up a flight of stairs, let alone go to shul.

It is as if we have dark contact lenses covering our eyes making everything look black and lifeless. When we look at ourselves, all we see are our countless mistakes. The same is true when we look at others. It seems to us that we are truly pessimistic "by nature." It appears as if we were born to be depressed.

We try different methods of escape – pills, drugs, alcohol, and therapy. Sometimes it seems like something works for a little while, but then our good old "friend" depression comes right back. After a while, we lose hope and just try to keep ourselves as distracted as possible so that we won't have time to feel the emotional and spiritual pain that we are suffering.

The Rebbe's Prescription: The light from one mitzvah can push away all the sadness and inspire you to serve Hashem with joy! (Based on Likutei Mohoran, 282)

Our biggest sin is that we focus too much on our mistakes.

While it may be true that we've made mistakes and sometimes committed grievous sins, G-d forbid, our biggest mistake is that we focus and dwell on our sins day and night. We constantly go over them in our mind, until we convince ourselves that we are really bad people and we are rotten at the core. Once we've established this fact, we fulfill our own self-prophecy and do more sins, usually more severe ones than the ones we originally made.

Thus, even though we should try never to sin, the worst possible thing we can do is to become depressed from our sins. This causes us to get caught in a vicious cycle of transgression and guilt which leads us to complete spiritual destruction. After a while, we identify so deeply with our depression that it seems like it is an integral part of us. Our self-esteem falls so low that it becomes habitual for us to look at ourselves negatively, that we can't believe that there is a way out. But, the Rebbe has a way…

Even the worst sinners have done mitzvos, and these good deeds are an eternal light.

Rebbe Nachman says that even if we are so wicked that we've committed the most atrocious sins, we still have some good in us. Even if we've transgressed the worst possible prohibitions in the Torah, G-d forbid, nonetheless, we must have done something good in our lives. Maybe once, we gave a dollar to tzedakah. Maybe once, we said *Krias Shema*. Maybe once, we put on a tallis or tefillin, even just for our bar mitzvah.

Although these good deeds seem completely wiped out by our countless sins, the truth is that they are eternal. Even the worst transgressions cannot destroy the light of one tiny mitzvah. Every good deed that we've done gives Hashem incredible *nachas*, regardless of our mistakes. These mitzvos are the key to saving ourselves from the darkness...

We must search for a mitzvah that we've done and then focus solely on its brilliant light.

Therefore, even if it may be hard at first to find a mitzvah since we are so accustomed to looking at our negative side; we have to search with all of our strength. We have to look persistently in every aspect of our lives until we're able to find something good that we've done; however small it may be.

Once we find something, although it may feel counter-intuitive, just for a moment we should try to look only at this mitzvah and nothing else. We're not lying to ourselves and pretending that we haven't messed up, rather, we're choosing to focus just on this one good deed for now.

When we start looking at it closely and examining it, we begin to see that it is shining with a brilliant light. It is a precious jewel which rests on Hashem's crown itself. The whole entire world was created just for this mitzvah. This mitzvah completely changed our soul. At that moment, we listened to Hashem and followed His Torah. From this physical world of darkness and desire, we were able to do something for the King of all Kings, the Master of the Universe!

Although most of us don't understand all of the secrets of Kabbalah; just the fact that we know that it teaches us that every mitzvah affects this world and all the higher worlds in a tremendous way, is enough for us to cherish our one mitzvah and grasp its true value.

Even if our mitzvah is far from perfect, we must look only at its goodness.

However, very often when we start to examine our mitzvah, we see that it is also far from perfect. In fact, it may have some big gaping holes. For example, we gave money to tzedakah, but in our heart we didn't really want to. We were even a little upset at the time.

Another example is that we put on tefillin, but then we schmoozed for a half an hour and maybe even said some *lashon harah*. Or, we davened *minchah*, but we spent most of the time calculating our finances.

When we see the imperfections in our mitzvah, our *yetzer harah* entices us to just throw the whole thing in the trash. The *yetzer harah* tells us that this mitzvah is completely worthless with all of its blemishes. He wants to destroy what little hope we have gathered to find something good about ourselves. But, we have to fight him back!

We have to ignore all of the darkness surrounding our mitzvah. Though it may seem like the mitzvah was mostly bad because of its impure intentions and myriad of mistakes; nevertheless, there must be some good in it as well. So, once again, we must block out all of the darkness and just focus on the light. At the end of the day, after working many hours to make a living, we took our own hard-earned money badly needed for ourselves, and we gave it to another person. This is amazing! The Sages say that the mitzvah of tzedakah is as valuable as the entire Torah. So with those few coins, we fulfilled all of Hashem's commandments.

When we examine the mitzvah of tefillin, we should see that we put Hashem's crown itself on our head. We gave the ultimate splendor to the Creator of the universe.

When we davened *minchah*, we stopped in the middle of our day from whatever it is that we were doing, and stood before the Holy One, Blessed is He, in prayer.

We should continue searching for more mitzvos and appreciate their beauty.

By looking only at the good in our mitzvah it begins to radiate with light. This light shines into our soul and we start to feel a little bit better. We begin to have a little bit of hope. But we shouldn't stop with just one. We certainly have done other mitzvos in our life as well. So, we should look and search very hard until we find another one, and then another one. We should examine each one of these mitzvos and see their incredible brilliance and beauty. And even if they too were imperfect, we should completely disregard their blemishes and focus on their amazing goodness.

Through this, we come to true happiness and spiritual inspiration.

What happens after this is truly remarkable… We begin to feel like a huge weight has been lifted off our shoulders. The storm cloud of depression hanging over our head begins to dissipate and then, it is gone altogether. We begin to feel like a different person. We begin to feel happy. That's right, happy and joyful!

We begin to identify ourselves as essentially good people, and we no longer desire the pleasures of this world.

All of a sudden, we have new strength. We feel our soul burning brightly inside of us. We feel charged and energized to serve Hashem. We no longer associate ourselves with our mistakes and sins. We no longer identify ourselves as bad people who never succeed at anything, especially *avodas Hashem*. Rather, we realize who we truly are. We realize that we are the children of Avraham, Yitzchok, and Yaakov, of blessed memory. We realize that we have a holy *neshamah* which came straight from Hashem's throne of glory. We have a piece of G-dliness *mamash* inside of us. That's who we are.

The result of this is that we wake up from our sleep and start really doing teshuvah. We start separating ourselves from all of our negative attributes and physical desires; because we know that they're not for a holy Jew like us. Those things don't belong to us at all!

In addition, we find such joy in davening, learning and doing mitzvos that we have no interest in animalistic pleasures. We don't need pills to help us feel "fake" happiness, because we've got the real thing. We don't need drugs or alcohol to drown out our pain and suffering, because everything is okay now. Every ounce of laziness is gone from our being. We are alive. We are truly alive!

Our entire life becomes an extraordinary song, and especially our davening.

We start singing to Hashem day and night. Davening is no longer a heavy burden which we have to force ourselves to do. Rather, we're running to shul to put our tallis and tefillin, and daven to Hashem with a new song each day.

Every single step that we take on the way to yeshivah or to work becomes like a new note in a wondrous niggun. By the time we arrive at our destination, we've completed a long and exquisite melody. As we sit in our office typing on a computer, it is as if we're playing a brilliant composition on a grand piano.

We begin to see that the entire creation around us is also singing an incredible song. We start to hear the birds chirping and to see the beauty of the trees swaying in the wind. Even in the midst of a busy city, we notice that the sound of the subway or train taking off makes the notes of a song.

When we sit down to learn Torah, our head is clear and free of all its previous grogginess. Learning becomes so much more *geshmak*, since; we're able to use our mind to think deeply. We're able to grasp new concepts and *sugyahs* so quickly, that it almost seems as if we must have learned them before.

We enjoy life; and we especially enjoy serving Hashem.

Our *yetzer harah* uses a guilt-trip to stop us from focusing on our mitzvos.

However, since this practice of seeing our good points (by focusing on them and treasuring them) fundamentally changes our entire experience of this world and completely transforms our *avodas Hashem*; we must know that there is an unbelievable amount of opposition from our *yetzer harah*. It is *mamash* a war in which the Other Side will do anything to sabotage us and prevent us from succeeding.

The *yetzer harah*'s tactics are often very subtle and mischievous. He doesn't combat us by just telling us how we're such terrible people; because then we could simply respond by showing him our good points. Rather, he tricks us into thinking that it's a mitzvah to be depressed. He says, "How do you think that you can do teshuvah by neglecting your sins and only focusing on the good. If you really want to do teshuvah, you have to confess your sins to Hashem with sincere remorse and regret. Only then will you be able to change and come closer to Him."

This sounds so logical to us – after all, it is what the Rambam writes in Hilchos Teshuvah (Halacha 1). So we forget about our good points and start trying to beat ourselves up for all of our mistakes in order to do what we think is "real" teshuvah. What follows is perhaps our greatest fall into complete and utter sadness and bitter darkness, the likes of which we've never known before. Since we think that we're doing a "mitzvah" by focusing on our transgressions and trying to feel deep regret for them; it seems to us that the harsher we are with ourselves, the better. We want to do the mitzvah a thousand percent… The problem is that it is not a mitzvah; rather, it is a mischievous trick of the *yetzer harah* to get us to completely destroy ourselves.

When we're strong we can do *vidui* but until then, we must build ourselves up.

We must understand that there is a time and a place for what the Rambam says. When we already have some spiritual strength in us, and we know that Hashem loves us and we are essentially good people; then, we can try to remove our sins by feeling regret and confessing to Hashem. When we already identify ourselves as holy Jews who give Hashem unbelievable *nachas* and we're happy with our good points; then, it is incredibly beneficial to make an account of our sins and purify ourselves in order to reach the next level.

However, when we're totally broken inside and we've sunken to the lowest depths of sadness and despair; the practice of focusing on our sins and feeling remorse for what we've done is only a trick of our *yetzer harah* to get us to finish off his job of total destruction.

So, we have remain strong against the *yetzer harah*, and completely disregard the guilt-trip he tries to pull on us. At another time, G-d willing, we will be able to do a confession, but right now is only a time for us to heal our soul. Right now is the time to build ourselves up. Right now is the time for us to see our incredible value and splendor in Hashem's eyes. Right now is the time for us to find true inner strength by focusing only on our mitzvos.

We can't let our *yetzer harah* make us think that looking at our good points is arrogant.

Another mischievous tactic of the *yetzer harah* is that he tricks us into feeling like focusing on our good points is very arrogant. He tells us, "You know what you've done, and now you want to pretend like you're such a tzaddik and you do so many incredible things for Hashem?!"

This also seems very logical. After all, we've really messed up, and most of the time we haven't listened to Hashem. Additionally, we wouldn't have been able to do even our mitzvos without Hashem's help. Our entire existence is dependent on Him and it is He Who gives us the strength to do His will. Isn't it arrogant for us to take credit for our good points?

But, this too, is a trick of the *yetzer harah*. While it is true that we should avoid being arrogant at all costs, the practice of focusing on our good points is very far from arrogance. We are not putting ourselves above any other person by bragging about our wondrous achievements. We're not pretending like we're perfect or better than anyone else. Rather, we're recognizing that, even though we've made mistakes, nevertheless there is immense value in every mitzvah that we've done. Even the daily mitzvos which all religious Jews practice are so precious in Hashem's eyes, that we should feel true happiness for doing them day in, day out.

In addition, we're not pretending like we've done anything all by ourselves without assistance from Heaven. Instead, we recognize that even though we were so far away from Hashem; we were able to awaken ourselves to have a desire to do His will and to try to follow in His ways, and He helped us to bring that desire into fruition. Indeed, the practice of recognizing our good points in no way brings us to arrogance.

If we simply can't find the good in ourselves, we should try to find it in others first.

However, sometimes the *yetzer harah* will not leave us alone. It seems to us that we are so accustomed to feeling guilty and pessimistic about ourselves that we simply can't escape him. It seems to us that every attempt that we make to focus our mitzvos is thwarted by a barrage of negative thoughts.

Our Sages say (Brachos 5b), "A person who is bound cannot release himself from prison." This means that sometimes it is almost impossible for us to break ourselves free of our depression and laziness. Every time we try to move towards the light and escape from our prison cell of darkness, we are countered by such an onslaught of bitter sadness that we feel completely bound and restricted from ever getting out. At such times, we should forget ourselves completely for a while and focus on finding the good in another Jew.

Though we naturally tend to see the negative traits in other Jews as well, as our pessimistic habits cause us to focus on their faults and to judge their sins; nevertheless, it is much easier for us to see the good points in someone else than it is to find them in ourselves. This is because when we look at ourselves, it is very hard for us to see the big picture. It is difficult for us to step out of our mind and see ourselves as a whole. However, with another person, since we observe them from far away, it is easier for us to see all of their different qualities, and to recognize the beauty of their mitzvos and *avodas Hashem*.

To understand this properly, let us take the following parable: Two people painted large pictures of themselves on opposing walls. Each painting was a fantastic masterpiece, except that both artists made mistakes in specific places. However, both of the painters were extremely disappointed with their work. They stood a few inches away from their painting, looking only at their mistakes and feeling terrible about what they'd done. Since they were standing so close, it seemed that no matter what they did, all they could see were the imperfections.

However, when each painter turned around and saw his friend's picture, because of his distance from the picture, he was able to admire its beauty and excellent skill. Since he was standing far away from his friend's painting, he hardly noticed the mistakes at all. So, each artist complimented the other and encouraged his friend to step back from his own picture and see its overall good qualities.

So too, when we look at ourselves, we are examining ourselves from such close proximity that our *yetzer harah* causes us to see only our faults and sins. It often feels impossible to step back and view ourselves in a positive light. However, when we look at other Jews, it is often easier to see their good qualities and focus on them. Despite a person's sins, he does countless mitzvos as well, of which each one is an invaluable treasure. We can see that every Jew is beloved by Hashem and that each person is an integral member of the Jewish people.

But, if when we look at this person's mitzvos, we only see the mistakes that he makes, we must look deeper until we find something good in them. For sure, he's done something in his life that gave Hashem incredible *nachas*. We see that he keeps Shabbos and only eats kosher food. Amazing! Even if those mitzvos are far from perfection – he woke up late Shabbos morning and missed all of davening, or he stuffed kosher pizza down his throat like a cow – nevertheless, when we focus on the good in his mitzvos, we can see the wondrous splendor that he gives to Hashem. At the end of the day, he expressed incredible faith in Hashem and His Torah by observing the laws of Shabbos. At the end of the day, he kept his *neshamah* pure from serious contamination by not ordering pepperoni pizza at a non-Jewish restaurant. And just like with ourselves, we should look for one mitzvah after another until we're able to see that he's really a great person.

This has two long-term effects. Firstly, it affects the other Jew by helping him to identify with his good qualities and do teshuvah. Even if we don't actually say anything to him, just by looking at him in a positive light we can transform him. Our Sages say that the wicked eye (looking at someone negatively) can knock a person down. They also say the attribute of good is much greater than the attribute of evil. So without any doubt, by simply focusing on the good in someone else we can have a tremendous impact on them for the better. This is true, all the more so, if we actually say an encouraging word to strengthen and lift them up.

Secondly, it has an incredible effect on us. By helping another Jew out of his darkness, we awaken within us the ability to do the same for ourselves as well. By seeing the good in someone else, we find the strength and courage to see it in ourselves, and it becomes increasingly easier for us to focus on our mitzvos and to do teshuvah. We're able to step back from our own picture and see that, overall, it is really a fantastic work of art and we should be very pleased with all of our successes. By helping another Jew out of his imprisonment, we too can find a way out of ours.

We are all sweet, juicy pomegranates, filled with amazing mitzvos!

This idea of focusing on our good deeds can be summarized by what the Sages say (Eiruvin 19a): "Even the sinners of Yisroel are full of mitzvos like a pomegranate." When we examine this comparison between a Jew and a pomegranate, we can understand the importance of finding and cherishing our good points.

Out of all the sweet and delicious fruits, the pomegranate is perhaps the least popular amongst the *goyim*. You may find pomegranate juice in a non-Jewish store outside of Israel, but you will rarely find a whole pomegranate. This is not because they spoil quickly; in fact, pomegranates keep for a very long time. It is also not because of the price of importation, since the *goyim* have no problem spending tons of money on imported dates, olives, and coconuts, etc.

Rather, the reason is because it is not so easy to eat a pomegranate. Even after it is cut open, it is very hard to extract the kernels from the waste. There are many different methods for getting them out, but at the end of the day, none of them are as easy as peeling a banana. And even after the kernels are extracted, there is still another unpleasant crunchy seed inside of them. Why bother with so much trouble just for the small amount of sweet juice?

However, our Sages paint for us quite a different picture. They teach us that every little bit of good is invaluable. They teach us that we should treasure the sweetness of our mitzvos even if they are surrounded on the inside and outside by garbage. Even if we open ourselves up and see that we are mostly waste because of our countless sins; we must extract the "fruits" of our good deeds and focus on them. We should admire every single kernel of goodness that is inside of us.

And even when we see that on the inside of that kernel of a mitzvah there is also some *shmutz* and it is far from perfect, nonetheless, we must recognize the sweetness that is in that mitzvah. Thus, we make a berachah and enjoy it, together with its waste. This is the deeper understanding of why the Sages compare a Jew to a pomegranate.

To summarize, the practice of finding and focusing on the good points in ourselves and others is completely life-changing. Through this, we can break ourselves free of our dark and bitter depression, and find true happiness and strength. Although the *yetzer harah* will do everything he can to prevent us from seeing our good, by following the advice of Rebbe Nachman and never giving up; we will be able to break free of our sadness and run to serve Hashem with joy!

Chapter Ten

The Illness: No matter what I do, I can't find a way to be happy.

Happiness is, perhaps, the most elusive thing in the entire world. One could have all the riches he could ever imagine, and still be utterly depressed. One could have a beautiful, healthy family, and still be completely broken on the inside. One could even be a huge *talmid chacham* with incredible knowledge of the Torah, and still feel depressed about his life.

We try many remedies to see if they will make us happy; but it seems that no matter what we do, we simply can't get rid of the dark, cold, and bitter sadness which we feel. We ask all of our rabbonim; we go to multiple therapists. They all tell us things that, in theory, seem like good ideas. But when we try to put their ideas into practice, the result is always the same: we remain stuck in the mud of our depression.

Sometimes, we try a pill or a certain method which appears to be helpful for a little while. Unfortunately, after a period of time, we run out of gas and we're back on empty. So, we convince ourselves that there really is no way to find joy in our lives, and we succumb to our depression.

The Rebbe's Prescription: Sometimes, you simply need to "fake it till you make it," and just do something silly. (Based on Likutei Halachos, Nefilas Apayim 4)

Through happiness, we can reach our greatest potential in avodas Hashem.

Most of us would agree that happiness is our ultimate goal. When we're happy, we're able to serve Hashem on a very high level. We can cast away all the clouds of confusion and doubt which cover our mind. All of our fears about the future and our guilt about the past which weigh us down and prevent us from davening and learning, are completely obliterated in a moment of true simcha.

Then, with a clear mind, we're able to focus on the words of our prayers and taste the sweet *deveikus* of *tefillah*. Instead of wasting hours a day with our head spinning around in circles from worry; we are able to sit down and learn every single moment we can find. We're able to fill our day with *avodas Hashem*, going from one mitzvah to the next without any distractions.

Since our thoughts are free of the burden of doubts and questions, we don't get so tired all the time and we need much less sleep. We are very productive at work and we get things done very quickly and efficiently. We can climb the social ladder easily and become very successful at whatever we put our mind to.

Additionally, when we're able to experience the love and awe of Hashem through our attachment to His Torah and mitzvos with joy; the physical desires of this world cease to attract us. The happiness and contentment of being an *eved Hashem* is so much better!

Because of the influence of non-Jewish culture, many of us are very far from true happiness.

However, most of us would admit that we're very far from achieving true happiness. In fact, we feel like it's almost impossible for us to find simcha in our lives. *Indeed, if this is our ultimate goal and* the key to our physical and spiritual success; isn't it strange that only a fraction of us are able to attain it? We are all working very hard to find happiness, so why are we not seeing any results from our efforts?

The reason is that we're not getting the right advice. The non-Jewish world around us is pumping us full of misinformation: They're telling us that the way to happiness is through making lots of money, buying the fastest sports cars, and eating the juiciest steaks... They're telling us that the way to happiness is through drinking, drugs, and pills... They're telling us that the way to happiness is to "live it up" in this world.

At first glance, it appears to us like they are right: It seems as if they really do have it good; it seems as if they're always smiling and flying high. It seems that way, but it's not that way...

Really, they're suffering more deeply than we could ever imagine. Even though they have a lot of money, they are so greedy that it's never enough... They're constantly jealous of their associates who have even more than them: They only have two vacation houses, and the other guy has got four. He even has one in Switzerland, which he flies to for an entire week each month!

Since they're not faithful in their marriages, they cannot build any real connection with their spouses. They both know that really they're just using each other to satisfy their own desires. In addition, most wealthy *goyim* do not have any real friends; as anyone who has anything to do with them really just wants their money! So, they end up feeling extremely empty and lonely.

If they have any children, they are so spoiled and arrogant that they give their parents terrible pain. Very often, their families completely fall apart and they break off contact with one another. They try to cover all this up by drinking, taking drugs, and popping pills, but once the high is over; they feel so bad that they become suicidal. Even with all the incredible new discoveries of modern medicine which lengthen our days on this earth; the life expectancy rate in the U.S. is declining rapidly because the rising amount of suicides. Clearly, the *goyim* are not good examples for us on how to achieve happiness.

Real joy and contentment can only come through our attachment to Hashem and His mitzvos.

Rather, we must know that true happiness can only come from our spiritual pursuits. Only through serving Hashem can we find contentment with our lives; since we know that we're fulfilling our purpose in this World and preparing ourselves for the Next One. Every single mitzvah that we're able to do, as well as every single word of Torah and *tefillah* is worth millions of dollars in our spiritual bank account. Every single religious Jew has infinitly more wealth than Bill Gates! That's a reason to be happy!

Just by keeping the basic halachah, we're sustaining the entire physical and spiritual World. Just by saying berachos on our food; we're fixing all of Creation. Just by saying kiddush on Shabbos, we're testifying to the world the Oneness of Hashem. Through our prayers, we have a personal relationship with the Master of the Universe. We are His beloved children, for whom He created everything, and to whom He gave His most treasured gift. *Amazing!* These are true reasons to be happy.

Sometimes, our sadness is so severely ingrained inside us that we can't get away from it.

However, even though we know that we should be able to find happiness through our mitzvos and *avodas Hashem*; nevertheless, many of us find it *very* hard to do so. We are so lost in exile among the *goyim*, that we can't appreciate what a mitzvah really is. We are so lost in our physical desires, that we can't get any spiritual enjoyment from davening *Shemoneh Esrei* .

Indeed, our depression seeps so deeply into our bones that we can't find a way out. It becomes so attached to our body and mind that we feel like we have no ability to escape it. We feel like we're tied down with heavy chains and stuck inside a strait jacket. We sincerely try to strengthen ourselves to be optimistic. We give it all we've got to see ourselves positively, and to be happy with the fact that we believe in Hashem and we follow His holy mitzvos; but we still can't shake off our sadness. It feels as if it's stuck to us like leeches all over our skin. It seems almost impossible for us to connect with true simcha.

At such times, we must force ourselves to act silly.

Nevertheless, Rebbe Nachman *z"tl* shows us a way out. He says (Sichos HaRan, 20) that when our depression is so deeply ingrained in us, the only way to release it is to "fake it 'til we make it." We must force ourselves to pretend that we're really happy. We must imagine as if it's Purim and it's our turn to do a "*shpiel.*" We can get up and do a funny dance. We can speak in a strange voice or comically imitate a different accent. We can read from a joke book, or tell our own jokes or we can just sing a silly song. Much like a badchan (Jewish jester) at a wedding; we can lighten our own mood with all types of humor.

Despite the fact that inside we are still really depressed and we're just acting like we're happy on the outside; by pretending to be joyous and funny, we can quickly remove the heaviness that is stuck in our body and soul. By putting our suffering aside and forcing ourselves to be silly and playful, we can break ourselves free of all our chains and get out of our darkness. It is usually a matter of minutes before our "faking it" becomes "making it," and we actually start to feel happy.

When we're in exile, we must connect to the simcha which is with us in exile.

Reb Nosson *z"tl* explains (see Likutei Halachos, Nefilas Apayim 4) why this method is so effective. He says that much like the Shechina which follows us into exile no matter how far we may fall, so too the joy of a Jew – which really is the Shechina Itself (see Likutei Mohoran I, 24) – follows us into our exile. This means that it becomes disguised in the humorous actions which make us externally happy. This happiness is an "exiled" happiness, since it is not coming from a deep internal place.

While on the one hand this is a lack, on the other hand it is an incredible benefit; since we can always access this disguised simcha, even when we are lost in the external world and we have no way to directly reach true internal happiness. In such a low place of physical and spiritual exile, using humorous and silly actions is the *only* way that we can find to be happy.

Our external happiness can lead us to the true happiness of being a Jew.

Once we tap into this superficial joy and we attach ourselves to the simcha with us in exile, then we free ourselves from our exile altogether. This is expressed clearly in the verse (Yishaya 55), "And through happiness, you will go out [of exile]." Similarly, we say in *Mussaf* on Shabbos, "May it be Your Will, Hashem, that you should lift us up through simcha to our [holy] land."

So, we see that by faking happiness and doing something silly, even if it's completely insincere; we can liberate ourselves from the exile of our constricted consciousness and free our mind and body from its depression. We can shake off – literally and figuratively speaking – the heavy sadness that has sunken into our bones and grabbed ahold of our thoughts.

Then, once we're out of our exiled state of mind, we can connect to the true joy of being a servant of Hashem. We can find the real, internal happiness that is in every single mitzvah and word of Torah. We can rejoice over the incredible blessing that Hashem chose us to be Jews. We can remember that every good deed that we do is fulfilling the purpose of Creation and giving us great reward in the World to Come, and with this, we can fill our heart with true joy.

In order to be silly, we must first realize that we're not so big and important.

However, this advice of Rebbe Nachman – to act silly and humorous – is in itself very hard for us to fulfill. We are not little kids anymore. We are grown-ups! These things are far beneath our dignity. How can we lower ourselves to such an immature level?

To overcome this obstacle, we must take ourselves off our lofty pedestal. It's true that we are adults and we have the capability to think about very complex things and perhaps, we even have very important work that we do in the world. Maybe, we're the president of a business or head of a yeshivah or kollel. Nevertheless, we're still suffering in exile. We have not reached the level of true tzaddikim who have completely cleansed themselves of all their depression, bad *middos*, and desires, and attained the highest levels in *avodas Hashem*. Since our tzaddikim are not living in any spiritual exile whatsoever; perhaps, they don't need to go down to such low places to bring themselves to simcha. We, on the other hand, are struggling with our temptation for money, food, and *kavod*, etc. We're struggling with our anger and arrogance. We're far away from true attachment to Hashem and His service in every aspect of our lives. We are *still* in physical and spiritual exile.

By recognizing our place, however, we can find our way out. By being honest with ourselves and letting go of our ego, we can accept the deep advice of Rebbe Nachman and use it to free ourselves from our exile. We know who we are and the sins we've committed, so we know that we're really not too big or important to act silly for a little while.

If we feel inhibited, we can use our children as an excuse to be playful.

But, even if we are willing to try to act comical; we often feel so self-inhibited and self-conscious that we can't actually bring ourselves to do it. Therefore, the first thing we should try to do is to use our small children as an excuse. Although it is considered absurd for an adult to act really silly, nevertheless, if we do it together with our kids it is more acceptable. We can pretend that we're doing it for their sake – as if we want to engage with them on their level – while inside, we really have another intention: to make ourselves happy.

For example, we can have conversations with our kids in gibberish. We can pretend to be wild animals and growl and roar with them. We can sing the funny kids' songs that they like. We can even try to improvise new words to the certain tunes they like and make up comical rhymes. We can read them amusing books, or tell silly stories. We can have a mock "laughing contest," and see who can come up with the funniest laugh!

With all of these things and more, we can overcome our inhibitions – express our silly selves and free ourselves from our own bitter darkness – while covering our tracks as if we are simply being playful parents!

We can also go to a place where we're alone and let our silliness out.

Another thing we can do is go to a private place where we won't feel embarrassed by other people. (In fact, if there aren't any children around, our silly actions should be done specifically in private; since they may not be considered proper public conduct and may tarnish the image of a Jew in today's society.)

When we're all alone in a room, a car, or another discrete place, what happens there will stay private and no one else will find out about it. This can ease our self-consciousness and help us feel free to joke around.

We can't stop to think: Rather, we must simply act spontaneously.

Nevertheless, even in such a situation, most of us are so unaccustomed to acting comical and silly that it's still very hard for us to actually do it. We are so self-inhibited that even when we're by ourselves that it's difficult for us to watch ourselves doing such crazy things.

The way to overcome this obstacle is to force ourselves to get up and do it. Once we start to think about what we're going to do and how to do it, then our analytical mind kicks in and we get lost in questions, doubts, and inhibitions. After this, our depression takes over and we convince ourselves that there's no way we could actually act in such a bizarre way. We've never done such a thing before in our entire lives, except maybe once or twice when we had too much to drink.

Therefore, we must simply act as though we are drunk! A drunken person doesn't think or analyze his actions. He doesn't care about what other people think, never mind what he thinks of himself. He just does what he wants. This is exactly what we must do, but without the aid of alcohol. Without thinking, we must get up and start imitating a chicken dance. *"Bok, bok, bok!"* Whatever we instinctively feel like doing, we must force ourselves to do it without having any doubts or second-guessing ourselves.

(Note: Of course, we shouldn't do anything that is prohibited by the Torah, G-d forbid, such as cursing, saying dirty words, or anything that is immodest, etc.)

Once we've achieved true silliness, then we should connect the simcha to its source: Torah and mitzvos.

As a result, we are able to lift ourselves up from the depths of our depression to a state of happiness in a matter of minutes. We are able to break ourselves free from our bonds of slavery, and liberate our mind from its clouds of confusion and sadness. However, as mentioned before, we shouldn't stop there. Rather, we should connect to this happiness, which has been exiled together with us, to the True Source of *all* happiness – being a Jew who has the holy Torah and mitzvos. We should remember who we really are – Hashem's very own children.

In other words, immediately after our private silly session, we should open a *sefer* and learn, or do a mitzvah. We should take our new freedom and use it to serve Hashem. With this, we can sustain our state of happiness and use it to get even closer to our Creator. We can take advantage of our clear mind to strengthen our attachment to Torah and *tefillah*. We can climb even higher in every aspect of our lives and escape our spiritual exile.

And if we fall back down, it's not a problem. We now have the recipe for success... Now, we know just how to "fake it 'til we make it."

Chizuk in Teshuvah

Chapter Eleven

The Illness: Whenever I try to do teshuvah, I usually end up falling further away from Hashem.

It's Elul. With just one month left until the Day of Judgement, we're all on our best behavior. We try to wake up a little bit earlier and make it to *shacharis* on time. We try to focus harder while we're learning, and we even try to squeeze in an extra *shiur* here and there. In addition, we realize that we need to work on our physical desires and bad *middos*, so we choose something we want to fix and set to it.

Some of us are actually able to continue pushing ourselves to improve all the way to Yom Kippur. But after that, we feel like we've accomplished everything that we need to do, so we can relax and have a nice *Bein Hazmanim*. We stop reaching for more, and very often we fall back into the same place that we were before.

However, most of us don't even make it so far. After a week or so into the month of Elul, we have a day where things are just not going right. We stayed up too late the night before and slept in past our alarm, so we missed our regular *shacharis* minyan. Then, after showing up late to our *chavrusah*, we were so tired that we had to put our head down and rest. Later that day, we got into a nasty argument with our spouse or roommate and completely lost our temper.

All of sudden, our dreams of Elul and teshuvah come crashing down before us. We completely lose our inspiration. We feel even more depressed and disappointed than before, and we fall even further away from Hashem.

The next year when Elul comes around, we give it another go, but with the same results. After a few years, we stop trying to do teshuvah. *Why should we cause ourselves to become worse than we already are?* We feel like we must accept that we can't do teshuvah and it is not possible for us to make a lasting transformation.

The Rebbe's Prescription: At the same time that you must try to reach higher, you must also strengthen yourself and hold yourself up. (Based on Likutei Mohoran I, 6)

Teshuvah is not measured by results. Rather, it is a path that we're constantly striving to walk along.

There is a common mistake that we make when trying to do teshuvah. We think that it's all or nothing; we either "did" it or we "didn't" do it. When we succeed in accomplishing our goal without any mistakes, we think that we've arrived. That was it, we "did" teshuvah. Period. Now, we can relax and give ourselves a nice reward for having worked so hard. We become complacent and let go of our desire to improve.

On the other hand, most of us feel like we're never able to "do" anything. As hard as we try, we don't see any results from our efforts. Maybe for a little while we're able to do more for Hashem, but then we fall and all of our progress is completely wiped out.

Rebbe Nachman teaches us that in order to do teshuvah, we must change our idea of what teshuvah really is. Teshuvah is not about results. It is not like a math test that we mark off "passed" or "failed." Rather, teshuvah is like a path that we're constantly traveling on. No matter how far we go on this path, we never reach our final destination before we leave this world. However, at the same time, even if we're only able to move a tiny little bit, we're still progressing on the path. Our goal is not to get stuck or go backwards. Instead, we want to constantly be in the process of moving along this path, no matter how fast or slow we're able to go.

To attach ourselves to the process of teshuvah, we must constantly yearn to improve.

Rebbe Nachman explains that in order to accomplish our goal and walk on the path of teshuvah, we must develop two skills. Firstly, we must always have a desire to go further. We must always yearn to transform our ways and attach ourselves more and more to Hashem and His mitzvos.

For example, we should try to wake up earlier, and make more time to learn Torah. We should try to daven with more *kavanah*, and overcome our habitual anger, arrogance, and other bad *middos*. In addition, we should express our desire to change in personal prayer to Hashem and beg Him to help us remove our physical desires and laziness and know Him in all ways…

This longing and yearning must be a constant part of our lives, since there is always further to go and higher levels for us to achieve. Even the greatest tzaddikim of all time did not reach absolute perfection. Moshe Rabbeinu, for example, was able to grasp forty-nine gates of wisdom, but the fiftieth he was unable to grasp (see Nedarim 36a). Similarly, Shlomo Hamelech writes (Koheles 7:23), "I said I will become wise, [but wisdom] is [still] distant from me."

In addition, the verse in *Tehillim* says (145:3), "[Hashem's] greatness is beyond measure." This means that even if we've reached very high levels of knowledge of the Torah, both in the Talmud and Kabbalah, and even if we daven with the utmost *kavanah* and perform the mitzvos with the most extraordinary *deveikus*, and even if we are recognized by all as a true tzaddik, we still must yearn for more and try to improve.

All the more so, it is important for those of us who are very distant from these exalted levels in Torah and mitzvos, not to become complacent in our achievements and constantly strive for growth. This aspect is essential for us to continually progress along the path of teshuvah.

We must hold ourselves up in the face of disappointment and do whatever we can for Hashem.

However, there is a second, equally important aspect to teshuvah which is absolutely crucial for us to succeed. It is the ability to hold our ground when we're struggling and be happy with even the smallest achievements. In the process of trying to change our ways, there are always countless difficulties and setbacks. Every time we try to pick ourselves up and move along the path of teshuvah, we are inevitably met with obstacles that prevent us from achieving our goals. These obstacles often seem completely insurmountable. It seems to us as if we did everything we could, but in Heaven there is a decree that does not allow us to change.

This apparent decree is due to our many sins in this lifetime and in previous incarnations, which cause any attempt to move forward to be met with incredible counterforce. Our *yetzer harah* does let go so quickly and becomes entrenched in us. Our mistakes in the past hold us back and block us from improving.

We get *so* disheartened because of this, that not only do we stop trying to move forward; rather, we fall back even further than we were before. We feel like we gave it our best effort, but Hashem just doesn't want us to succeed, G-d forbid. So, we sink into darkness and despair.

Therefore, in the process of teshuvah, we must spend long periods of time simply holding our ground and strengthening ourselves to continue doing all the little things we can for Hashem.

Even if there is an impenetrable wall blocking our path and preventing us from reaching our goals and progressing quickly, we must not turn around and go backwards. Instead, we must encourage ourselves to take the small steps that we are capable of. Even though we aspire to achieve so much more, a little bit is also good. It's not all or nothing… Hashem loves every tiny effort that we make to serve Him.

For example, even if we can't learn as many hours a day as we had hoped, we shouldn't get down on ourselves. Rather, we should do whatever learning we can and strengthen ourselves with the faith that every word of Torah gives Hashem great *nachas*.

If we really want to be able to start davening with *kavanah*, we have to see that even our *tefillos* full of foreign thoughts is invaluable to Hashem. Just the fact that we took time out of our day from pursuing our own desires is recognized by the Creator of the universe! If we want to give more tzedakah, we have to see that by giving just fifty cents is considered as if we've fulfilled the entire Torah.

By acquiring an expertise in both aspects of teshuvah, we will never get stuck or go backwards.

In order to continually be in the process of teshuvah, we must acquire an expertise in both of these aspects of teshuvah. In other words, although we must always strive for more – the first aspect of teshuvah, at the same time we must also be very happy with what we already have – the second aspect of teshuvah. This may seem like a contradiction, but it's really not. It means that we recognize our incredible value to Hashem, no matter how little we're able to do for Him; while at the same time we want to achieve the next level in *avodas Hashem*.

However, it is often very challenging for us to reach an expertise in both of these areas of teshuvah. Due to the source of our particular *neshamah*, we are naturally stronger in one area and weaker in the other. For example, some of us have an instinctive drive to constantly improve. We're never satisfied with staying in one place. Rather, we're always trying to transform and reach higher levels. On the other hand, we can't deal with disappointment and failure. When we don't meet our goals, we get so upset that we fall into utter despair and give up completely.

On the contrary, there are some of us who are naturally satisfied with who we are. Simply by davening *shacharis* every day, we know that we've done so much for Hashem. We are truly happy with our lot. However, we're lacking the yearning to push ourselves in *avodas Hashem*. We don't have the instinct to constantly fill our day with learning Torah and transforming our bad *middos*. We are too complacent to be able to progress on the path of teshuvah.

Therefore, each one of us must recognize our strengths and our weaknesses, and try our best to acquire the aspect of teshuvah that we're lacking. While not neglecting the aspect which we're more inclined to, we must build up the other aspect to be equally as strong.

With this method, we never get stuck or go backwards. There may be some days or periods of our life when we're able to jump leaps and bounds on the path of teshuvah. There may be other times when we're only able achieve smaller accomplishments. Nevertheless, we must never give up and we do what we can.

And even on the slower days, we must know that the little bit we're able to do is *just as important to Hashem* as the big achievements we make at other times. This is reflected in what the Sages say (*Menachos 110*), "The one who does a lot [is equal to] the one who does a little, as long as the intentions of his heart are for Heaven."

Although the simple understanding of this statement is that it refers to two separate individuals, nonetheless, it also refers to one person at two different times in his life. When we sincerely try to do our best, the days which are less productive are *equally as important to Hashem* as the more productive days.

From here we see that in Hashem's eyes, teshuvah has nothing to do with results. Rather, it is measured by our intentions and our desire to change, which gives us the strength to do whatever we're able any given moment.

Our obstacles to teshuvah are really just opportunities to prepare us for the next level.

When we're able to attain both of these aspects of teshuvah, then the obstacles we face along the path are actually very good for us. If Hashem would simply let us through to the next level in our weak state and didn't make us work for it, we wouldn't have the vessels to handle the increased level of *kedushah* and we would eventually fall even further away from Him. However, by constantly building our *ratzon* to change and making an effort to improve – the first aspect of teshuvah, while at the same time holding ourselves up from falling despite all of our disappointments – the second aspect, we create incredibly fortified vessels that can sustain us on a higher level.

Let's take, for example, trying to wake up earlier, whether it's to daven at sunrise, or to learn before *shacharis*, to try to pray before the *zman tefillah*, or to put on tefillin before sunset – each one of us according to his level. If Hashem made it easy for us to accomplish our goal and we were able to break the bonds of sleep without difficulty, then we might only be successful in doing so for a period of time. But since we never built our spiritual strength through yearning, prayer, and effort, we will never feel very sturdy in our new place. It won't feel solid and stable, until eventually, we will burn out completely and end up waking up even later than we did before.

Therefore, Hashem gives us incredible opposition to achieving our goal, both from our *yetzer harah* and from external obstacles, so that if we choose to hold on to our desire to change and wake up earlier, we will develop the capability to be truly prepared for the next level. Then, when we finally reach it, we will be able to make a lasting acquisition of that higher level, and be able to wake up consistently at the same time.

Through patience and humility, we will never fall into despair.

However, the process of overcoming our obstacles can be very discouraging at times. We can't see the benefit that we're getting from having to suffer through so much. We can't see any light at the end of the tunnel, so we lose hope of success. Therefore, we must understand that we're asking Hashem for the gold metal, like our Sages say (Yuma 86), "Teshuvah is able to reach [Hashem's] throne of glory." We want to achieve the ultimate purpose of creation – to be close to Hashem – so we must be patient.

We have to let go of our ego which tells us that if we're not immediately successful at reaching our goals, then we have no chance at all. Arrogance is the main thing that causes us to despair. We think that things should be easy and go our way, both in our physical and spiritual endeavors. However, when they – more than often than not – don't go our way, we have to write off our failure with some excuse, in order to avoid damaging our ego.

For example, we have to say that we weren't born with the skills that we need to learn Torah or daven with deep *kavanah*. It's not due to a lack in us, rather, Hashem simply didn't give us the capability to do it. Or, in another example, we say that it's just not in our nature to be a generous person, so we give up on doing *chessed* at all.

Hashem doesn't make every Jew the same, and each one of us has more talent in one area and less in another; nevertheless, we all have a *neshamah* that is capable of serving Hashem through Torah, *tefillah*, and mitzvos, even if it's sometimes in very small ways.

Therefore, we must recognize that we really do have the ability to change our bad *middos*, just that we must first let go of our arrogance and accept that it may take some time. We must strive to achieve true humility by being patient with ourselves. This is itself the main teshuvah that we must do, like our Sages say (Sotah 5), "Someone who is arrogant, I (Hashem) cannot live together with him in this world." From here we see that the biggest wall between us and Hashem is our ego.

Thus, we should approach our obstacles to teshuvah, which embarrass us and reveal our true weaknesses, as the biggest blessings of Hashem, since they humble us and help us to build stronger vessels for the next level. In other words, we should rejoice over not being successful when trying to daven with *kavanah*. This shows that we don't care about our ego which is dependent on immediate results. Instead, we humbly recognize that we are far away from the *avodah* of *tefillah*, but at the same time we cherish our attempt and continue trying to improve.

You *can* teach an old dog new tricks!

Take the following parable: Imagine a young child who's learning the *Aleph Beis*. Each week he must work hard just to learn one letter, until by the end of the year he knows the whole thing. But even then, he still doesn't know any vowels and can't read at all. If the child were to think, "Why is it taking me so long? For sure by now, after an entire year, I should be able to learn *Tosafos* already!" Then, he would never succeed. However, since he's not so arrogant, he doesn't see it that way. Rather, he sees that each week he's able to learn a new letter, until finally he's learned them all. What an accomplishment! Amazing!

Thus, the child is able to progress in his learning, even though he takes it slowly, step by step. By continuing in this path, G-d willing, he will eventually have great success in learning *Tosafos*.

This is the way that each one of us must approach teshuvah. We must be very patient and see the incredible value of each small step that we're able to take. Instead of always focusing how much further we still have to go, we should concentrate on every tiny bit of progress that we've already made.

There is a common misconception that only children have the capability to learn something new, such as a foreign language, musical instrument, etc., but once someone has reached adulthood, they've lost the capacity to do so. However, this is completely and utterly false. Rather, it only seems this way because we give up too quickly in the face of adversity due to our low self-esteem and lack of patience with ourselves. But when we're able to be like a child and let go of our ego, then we can also pick up new skills and see real transformations in our spiritual work. Slowly but surely, we will be able to change our bad habits and progress on the path of teshuvah.

Even when we're faced with an impossible challenge, we must not lose our *ratzon*!

Nonetheless, there are times when the obstacles are so great, that no matter what we do, we're unable to move or change at all. We go through such hardships in our life – both physically and spiritually – that it is simply not possible for us to make any progress. The challenges and difficulties that we're faced with are so overwhelming, that we can't even take one step forward.

Indeed, there are times when our *yetzer harah* works so strongly against us that there's nothing we can do to stop him from pushing us back. It seems like everything in our life is going completely wrong, and we're drowning in the depths of the ocean without the ability to make it to shore.

At these times, we must know that we still have freedom of choice. Although we may not have the capability to overcome the challenges that are before us, we can choose to not give up and to keep trying. In these situations, the measure of our success is whether we despaired or we continued having the desire to do teshuvah. Even if the results of our efforts are completely fruitless, and on the contrary, we actually did worse than before, nonetheless, we must know that in these moments the test itself is only a test of our *ratzon* (see Likutei Halachos, Shabbos 7:54). Will we give up completely, or will we hold on as best we can?

For example, a man finds out that he just lost his job. His debt has already been piling up for years. He can't bear to face his wife with the bad news. Then, he gets stuck in terrible traffic on the way home. While sitting in the car, he gets a call that his son is failing yeshivah. Finally, he gets through the traffic and he stops in shul to daven *minchah* before going home.

His head is absolutely spinning with millions of worries, fears, and anxiety to the point that it is not within his capability to daven with *kavanah*. However, he still has the ability to choose… He can choose whether he's just going to throw his *minchah* in the garbage and be done with it, or whether he's still going to try. Even though he knows that it is almost impossible for him to succeed, since the obstacles are too great to overcome, nonetheless, his test in that moment is to see if he will still maintain his desire for Hashem.

And even if we end up taking steps backward on the path of teshuvah during these trying times, by doing our best to persevere and hold our ground; we will eventually receive incredible Divine assistance to help us transform and make huge leaps forward on the path. By being able to pick ourselves up time after time and not give up, we establish an unbreakable foundation of strength within ourselves, upon which we can then build up our *avodas Hashem* like a massive skyscraper.

By constantly strengthening our *ratzon*, we will inevitably experience the sweet smell of teshuvah.

To understand the nature of the process of teshuvah, Rebbe Nachman brings the following statement of our Sages (Yuma 38): "A person who is coming to purify himself receives [Heavenly] assistance. This is comparable to one who comes to purchase an exotic spice. Since the spice has such an amazing smell, [the clerk] tells him, 'wait and I'll measure it for you.'"

From here, we see that the process of doing teshuvah is like acquiring a heavenly spice. It is the most precious thing in the entire world – also known as Hashem's store. Therefore, Hashem the Clerk, so to speak, tells us to wait. He wants us to stand strongly in our place without budging one inch, and build up a strong yearning for it. He wants us to be humble and see that the outcome is in His hands alone. Nonetheless, by doing our part and striving for more, while at the same time holding ourselves up; it is only a matter of time until we receive our heart's desire and smell the sweetness of our teshuvah process.

Chapter Twelve

The Illness: I know Hashem exists, but I can't find Him in my life. I've fallen so far and I'm completely lost.

We all believe that Hashem created the entire universe from nothing, and He continues to create and sustain every living thing. We believe that His Presence fills the whole world around us and beyond. This is the basic principle of faith in one G-d. We also believe that Hashem gave us the holy Torah and that our fulfillment of His mitzvos is and always will be the sole purpose of creation. Additionally, we know that even if we have sinned, G-d forbid, Hashem is full of compassion and will give us a chance to do teshuvah; so that we can continue following His Torah.

However, we think – sometimes even subconsciously – that there is a limit to Hashem's compassion. There are certain mistakes that can always be fixed, but there are other transgressions for which we simply cannot do teshuvah. There are certain places which are distant from *kedushah* where Hashem's Presence can still be found; but there are other very contaminated places that are so far from any holiness, where there is no way that we could possibly find Hashem there.

When we fall into these places, our entire world goes dark. We feel bitter, cold, and utterly alone. We feel like we're being swallowed up by the forces of evil, without any hope of finding the light of Hashem.

The Rebbe's Prescription: Even in the darkest and most contaminated places Hashem can be found: You just have to search for Him. (Based on Likutei Mohoran II, 12)

Our primary purpose in this world is to reveal Hashem's *kavod* through fulfilling His mitzvos.

Rebbe Nachman says that on a surface level of understanding there is a boundary to Hashem's *kavod*, like the verse says (Yishaya 42), "And My *kavod*, to the Other [Side] I will not give." This means that there is a limit to Hashem's Presence, so to speak. There are places where, at first glance, Hashem's light cannot reach, so to speak.

Rebbe Nachman explains this reality by going back to the beginning of Creation. In the beginning, Hashem created the world with nine explicit utterances – correlating to the nine times that "*VaYomer*" is mentioned in the six days of Creation. These nine utterances all had the potential to reveal Hashem's *kavod* in the world through man's actions; each one according to the specific creation that it was made from. For example, when Hashem spoke and created the sky; this made it possible to reveal Hashem's *kavod* in the world through man's praises for Hashem's wonders around us. When Hashem spoke and created the plants and animals; this made it possible to reveal Hashem's *kavod* through our berachos on all the sustenance that Hashem gives us.

The same is true for every mitzvah of the Torah. Each mitzvah is a unique opportunity for us to reveal Hashem's *kavod* according to the specific aspects of that mitzvah. For example, Hashem created the wool of a sheep, so that we would reveal His *kavod* through the mitzvah of tzitzis. Hashem created the hide of a cow, so that we would reveal His *kavod* through the mitzvah of tefillin. This is our purpose in life – to reveal Hashem's *kavod* by following His Torah.

Since it is necessary for us to have a *yetzer harah*, it is almost impossible for us to never sin and fall away from Hashem's *kavod*.

However, if we were to be completely holy – without a *yetzer harah* – we would never get to reveal Hashem's greatness. In a place full of sunlight, a candle goes completely unnoticed. But in a dark room, even one small flame can illuminate the entire space.

So too, if we wouldn't have the potential to sin, our mitzvos wouldn't the light necessary to reveal Hashem's *kavod*. Therefore, Hashem gives us freedom of choice. By allowing us the capability to do evil, we can make Hashem great by choosing to do good. This is the purpose of our *yetzer harah*, as well as in the bigger picture; all the forces of darkness and contamination in the world.

Since we have freedom of choice, it is almost impossible that we will never fall. If we were always able to do the right thing; then we wouldn't have a fair fight with our *yetzer harah*, and we wouldn't any longer be able to reveal Hashem's *kavod*. So with this understanding, it is inevitable, in some way or another that we will end up in the contaminated places of our *yetzer harah*.

The problem is that these spiritually contaminated places were not created by the nine revealed utterances of Hashem ("*Va Yomer*"). Being that they are too far away from Hashem's *kavod*; He could not create them so explicitly, in order not to give them too much power in the world. So when we fall into these places, we are below Hashem's *kavod*, so to speak. We are in a place of total darkness, since it appears to us that there is no way to get out and connect to Hashem.

The most contaminated places receive their existence from the highest revelation of Hashem; albeit in a vastly hidden way.

Though, Rebbe Nachman explains that in truth, even these places must receive their existence from Hashem; because without Him, *how could they exist at all?* Nevertheless, as they are *so* contaminated;

Hashem sustains them in an extremely hidden way, in order not to give too much strength to the Other Side (as mentioned before). Therefore, instead of creating them through one of the revealed utterances; Hashem created them through the tenth, hidden utterance of the word "Bereishis."

This hidden utterance of "Bereishis" is on a much higher level than all of the nine revealed utterances. In fact, it is the source of the other nine utterances and of all the Creation that comes from them. However, since it is *so* incredibly exalted, its light cannot be revealed explicitly, because it would be much too powerful for this world to receive. Therefore, its light is clothed by the nine revealed utterances through which it is able to reach even the lower worlds.

Since the utterance of "Bereishis" is so hidden; it can directly sustain the places of contamination. As its light is not explicitly revealed, it does not destroy those places and doesn't give them too much power over the forces of *kedushah*.

There is never a reason to despair in the world!

So when we fall into these spiritual and physical places of darkness; *we should not lose hope!* Rather, we must remind ourselves that even though it seems like we're completely lost and we couldn't fall any further away from Hashem; this is simply not true. We must remind ourselves that, even though, it seems to us that we've messed up our lives so badly that it feels like we are beyond repair and that it seems like there is no way back to *kedushah*; this is simply not true. *In fact, on the contrary, we are closer to Hashem than ever!* The highest light of Hashem – the utterance of Bereishis – is right here with us, *mamash*. The only thing which can sustain us in such a disgusting and filthy place, is the source of all creation – the Bereishis utterance.

The only problem is that it is incredibly hidden. It is so concealed that we are completely unaware of it; we are not able to believe that it could exist in such contaminated places. Still, as Rebbe Nachman explains, it is there! So, *there is no reason to despair at all!* We are still very close to Hashem and we can find Him and get out of our garbage dump.

We must let go of our logical reasons for giving up and have faith in our tzaddikim.

So how do we find Him? The first thing we must do is strengthen our faith that Hashem is truly with us. We must throw away all our logical explanations for why we will never be able to get ourselves to attach to *kedushah* and believe – with all of our soul – in this particular teaching of Rebbe Nachman. We must let go of all of our "good reasons" to lose hope. We must realize that we know absolutely nothing. We are like tiny ants at the bottom of a huge mountain. We have a very limited perspective, and so we cannot fully understand the nature of our surroundings. However, the tzaddik at the top of the mountain is truly able to grasp our situation. He can see exactly where we are and recognize the essence of our location. Therefore, we must strengthen our faith in the teachings of the tzaddik, and allow him to help us rise above our darkness.

We must erase from our mind all our thoughts of despair which tell us that the tzaddik's Torah only applies to people on a higher level than us, and we must replace them with the truth that the tzaddik reveals to us: Hashem is with us even when we're completely lost in the world of temptation and sin.

By searching for Hashem's light from our darkness, we achieve the highest revelation of Hashem and with it, destroy the forces of evil.

Then, once we've strengthened our faith, we have to look for Hashem. Even if we're sitting in the middle of a spiritual garbage dump, covered in waste from head to toe; we must peck around like chicken looking for the bits and pieces of exalted *kedushah* hidden underneath all the refuse.

In other words, we have to build up a deep desire for Hashem. We have to long and yearn from the depths of our *neshamah* to find

Him. We have to search for Hashem with every ounce of courage that we have left. We have to call out to Him. We have to daven and plead with Hashem to help us find Him. We have to pray to Hashem with all of our *neshamah* and beg Him to reveal Himself to us. We have to scream to Him, from the bottom of our hearts: "Where are You, Hashem? Where are You?!"

What happens after this is truly remarkable… From the lowest spiritual place, we ascend up to the Source of all Creation. Through our deep search for Hashem's Presence, we are able to find Him even in our bitter darkness. In the end, not only do we find Hashem's light in our lives; but we also reveal to ourselves the most exalted place of Hashem's *kavod* – the hidden utterance of Bereishis.

Through our yearning and search for Hashem, we create a vessel that cannot be broken and that can receive His highest light. We make ourselves into a *kli* to reveal the Source of Hashem's *kavod* in this world. We attach ourselves to Hashem and destroy all the contamination covering over His incredible light.

The entire strength of the Other Side is only due to the *hiddenness* of the "Bereishis" utterance. It is because we don't realize our closeness to Hashem and because we think that His Presence can't be found in such a low place; that the Other Side is able to have any power over us at all. However, once we search for Hashem and find Him in our darkness; we cut these evil forces off from their source of existence (through the concealment of the light of Bereishis).

Through this search, our sins can become merits.

Thus, we go from the worst level of contamination – our countless sins and physical desires – to the highest level of purity – the source of Hashem's *kavod*. This is what is described in the *sefarim hakadoshim* as "*yerida tachlis ha'aliyah*" – our descent is for the purpose of going higher (see Likutei Mohoran I, 22).

Although we should never intentionally sin or cause ourselves to have a "*yeridah*," G-d forbid, nevertheless, as described above, it is inevitable due to our constant struggle with our *yetzer harah*. If we never fell and made mistakes; we wouldn't have real freedom of choice and be able to reveal Hashem's light. Therefore, each one of us (according our level) is bound to have *"yeridah"* at some point, and in our generation, they usually come on pretty regular basis. Sometimes, it seems to us like our entire life is one huge *"yeridah."*

Therefore, regardless of how it happens, when we find ourselves in the darkness of our sins; we must know that, right now, we have an opportunity to turn everything around and reach an even higher level than before. We have an opportunity to use our *"yeridah"* like a trampoline and bounce up to the most exalted places in *avodas Hashem*.

This is because before we sinned, we were living in a spiritual place of Hashem's revealed *kavod*. We were following Hashem's Torah and mitzvos, which are revelations of Hashem's light in the world, as explained above. However, when we sinned we fell below Hashem's *kavod*, so to speak, to a place of filth and contamination. We fell to a place where it seemed as if no *kedushah* could possibly exist there.

Nevertheless, there really is *kedushah* in such places; not only that, but the highest levels of *kedushah* and light are hidden there. So from such a place, we really have an amazing opportunity that we never had before: to reveal the hidden utterance of "Bereishis" – the highest light of Hashem!

Therefore, we must gather all the strength we can find to believe that now we can do something truly remarkable. Through our search for Hashem with all of our heart, we can transform our *yeridah* into an aliyah. In other words, we can turn our sins into merits. *What? This sounds ridiculous!* But it's true.

When we were able to strengthen ourselves after our sin and find an even higher light of Hashem than before, it turns out that our sin actually helped us come closer to Hashem. This is what the Sages say (Yuma 86), "Through teshuvah from love, one's sins become transformed into merits."

From the lowest level of *tumah* to the highest level of purity.

From here, we see the power of teshuvah. From here, we can understand how someone can go completely off the derech, but then turn his life around and create a deeper and more meaningful relationship with Hashem and His mitzvos than he ever had before. From here we can understand how someone can go from a serious drug addiction with seemingly no possibility of escape, G-d forbid, to an addiction to *tehillim* and *hisbodedus*. From here, we can understand how someone can go from a constant, relentless attachment to his smart phone, to a constant, relentless attachment to learning Torah.

From here we can understand how someone who didn't grow up with any Yiddishkeit at all, can have a spiritual awakening later on in his life and search for Hashem with all his strength until he finds his way to the Torah. From here, we can understand how a Jew can go from eating pork on Yom Kippur to a Rebbe in a yeshivah. From here, we can understand how a non-Jew who's living his life with absolutely no purpose, can look for the truth and become a holy Yid.

The main thing is our *ratzon*. We have to want Hashem to save us. We have to build our desire to find Him, and we must express our yearning to Hashem in words. Sometimes, it is not enough for us just to speak to Him and we must scream with all our heart and soul, "Where are You?!" Like someone who is looking in a dark room for something he knows is definitely there; we have to believe that He is really very close to us and He hears our sincere prayers. We have to know that He will reveal Himself to us, and lift us out of our spiritual destruction.

With this, we can reach the highest *deveikus* in Hashem and His *avodah*. With this, we are able to attach ourselves to the source of Hashem's *kavod* and merit to fulfill all His mitzvos and learn His Torah on a really high level. With this, we can do complete teshuvah and come truly close to our Creator.

Chapter Thirteen

The Illness: I've fallen so deep into physical desire that I can't feel the kedushah of my neshamah.

In this day and age, we are being tested more than ever before by the physical desires of the non-Jewish world. Although there may have been periods of time in past when the *goyim* were flagrantly immodest, lewd, greedy, and animalistic like they are today; nevertheless, in the past we could always find respite and *kedushah* in the seclusion of our own homes and separate communities. It was much easier for us to keep to ourselves and protect the sanctity of our tradition.

Today however, it is extremely challenging to isolate ourselves from the influence of the non-Jewish world. Many of us, for a number of reasons, have no choice but to live in cities and communities that are mixed with or immediately adjacent to *goyim*. Therefore, we are surrounded by screens, billboards, magazines, and advertisements, which convince us that the pleasures of this world are really what it's all about.

In addition, even if we are some of the lucky few who live in secluded, religious areas, due to the necessity of having the internet, our lives are deeply infiltrated by the *goyish* world. Our smartphones, computers, and other devices are filled with filthy garbage that makes our *neshamah* want to escape and hide. Because of this, even in the privacy of our own home we are not safe. This is unprecedented!

Sometimes, we fall to such low places that it's hard for us to see any difference between us and the *goyim*. We become so deeply assimilated into their culture of temptation that we don't feel the *kedushah* of our *neshamah* whatsoever.

The Rebbe's Prescription: By comparing yourself to a goy, you can see that your soul is shining with a brilliant holiness. (Based on Likutei Halachos, Reishis Hagez 4)

The main reason we fall is because we compare ourselves to the extraordinary *kedushah* of a Jewish *neshamah*.

Reb Noson of Breslov z"tl explains that the main reason we become assimilated into the modern culture of temptation is not because we compare ourselves to the *goyim*. Rather, on the contrary, the primary reason that we fall into the trap of the secular world is because we compare ourselves to the *kedushah* of a Yid.

The holiness of a Jewish *neshamah* is incredibly great. Our soul is a piece of Hashem Himself. We are Hashem's beloved children. He gave us His most precious gift. He chose us above all the nations of the world and even the angels of heaven, and gave us the Torah. In fact, the entire world was created just for Jewish souls to come into this world and keep the mitzvos. This is quite a tall order.

It is an amazing opportunity, but also a daunting responsibility. *What if we mess up?* There is so much riding on our freedom of choice that it can feel very heavy and difficult at times. The bar is set so high that it simply seems impossible for us to reach it.

We try to pull ourselves away from our physicality and attach ourselves to *avodas Hashem*, but no matter what we do; it seems like we're constantly falling short of who we should be and what we can achieve. Our potential is so great that when we look at ourselves honestly, it appears as if we're always extremely far away from the exalted purity of a Jew. It seems like we'll never be able to reach the level of *kedushah* that we know is appropriate for the children of Avraham, Itzhak, and Yaakov, may they rest in peace.

Because of this, our mood plummets. We give up all hope of being able to overcome our *yetzer harah*. We start to despair completely of achieving any attachment to the *kedushah* of our *neshamah* and we let go of even the little connection that we had to *avodas Hashem*. We feel like we have tried many times to be a good Jew, but the goal is just too lofty for us to attain.

We must recognize the vast differences between a Jew and a *goy*, and treasure every little bit of *yiddishkeit*.

However, we're making a huge mistake. While it is true that when we measure ourselves by the standard of holiness of a Jewish *neshamah* most of us fall very short, nonetheless, this is only a part of the truth — the part that our *yetzer harah* wants us to see. The flip side is that when we compare ourselves to a *goy*; we see quite a different picture.

Even if we've done very terrible sins and transgressed the Torah countless times to satisfy our desires, G-d forbid; we are still worlds away from the contamination of the *goyim*. Although it may seem to us that we act like animals just like the *goyim* do; when we actually line things up, this is very far from the truth.

For example, we have a *bris milah*. Even though we didn't do anything to merit such an awesome and holy mitzvah, nevertheless, Hashem had incredible compassion on us and brought us into His sacred covenant. Through this mitzvah alone, we are elevated light years above the animalistic nature of the *goyim*.

In addition, if we've kept Shabbos even once in our life, this too greatly distinguishes us from the *goyim*. For twenty-four hours we turned off our smartphones, stopped smoking cigarettes and other substances, and we didn't go shopping. *This is amazing!* In such a world of physical darkness, we detached ourselves even a little bit from our desires for the sake of a mitzvah. This is all the more so, if we keep Shabbos every single week!

Every time we put on a tallis we are wrapping ourselves in the light of the *chessed* of Hashem. Every time we put on tefillin we are placing Hashem's crown itself upon our head. Every time we say *Shema* – even if we missed the *zman* and we can't get the mitzvah, G-d forbid – we're unifying Hashem's name and proclaiming His oneness to the entire world. Even if we have barely any strength to daven and all we can do is recite the *Shemoneh Esrei* without any feeling or *kavanah* whatsoever, nevertheless we should be extremely happy. At least we're mumbling the holy words of the Sages, and not some lyrics to a lewd rock or hip-hop song.

Although we work all day with *goyim* and we share the same materialistic goals, when we stop during our lunch break to daven *minchah*, we completely separate ourselves from them. All the more so, when we take even a little bit of our hard-earned money and give *tzedakah*.

Even if we can't help ourselves from eating a sixteen oz. steak or downing a bottle of vodka, when we say a *berachah* before and afterwards, we completely separate ourselves from our non-Jewish counterparts. Even if we can't help ourselves from buying the most extravagant suit, when we wear it in honor of Yom Tov – even if our main intention is to show off – that suit is not the same as the one worn by our non-Jewish co-worker. Even if we can't stop ourselves from buying the fastest sports car, when we use it to go to shul or a wedding, it is not the same as the one our non-Jewish neighbor drives.

Even if we sit and watch the Super Bowl with our chips and salsa, juicy chicken wings, and cold Bud Light; even if we enjoy watching the cheerleaders, the half-time show, and most of all, a bunch of grown men smashing into each other as hard as they can, nevertheless, when it's all over and we open our siddur to daven *Ma'ariv*, we completely elevate ourselves from our non-Jewish football fans. With just that one *Krias Shema*, we show to the entire world and to ourselves that there is something more important in life than football. All the more so is this true for those of us living in Eretz Yisroel who, after staying up all night to watch the game, put on our tallis and tefillin and go to daven *shacharis* at *netz hachamah*. This is nothing short of *mesiras nefesh*!

Through this comparison we're able to find the light of our *neshamah* burning inside of us.

When we compare ourselves to a *goy*, every one of these mitzvos stands out and shines incredibly brightly. We see a completely different picture. We really aren't such bad people at all. We really are good servants of Hashem. We are covered from head to toe with the brilliant light of our Torah and mitzvos, like our Sages say (Eiruvin 19a), "Even the sinners of Yisroel are full of mitzvos like a pomegranate."

We begin to believe that we really do have a holy *neshamah*. We begin to see that there is something inherently different about us, like our Sages say, "Even a sinner of Yisroel is still called 'Yisroel.'" After everything that we've done, we're still Hashem's children.

We begin to see that there is a fundamental part of us that has no desire for this world. There is a piece of G-dliness inside of us that only wants Hashem.

We begin to identify with our *neshamah*, and not with our animalistic self. We begin to hope that we can lift ourselves out of our physical temptations. We begin to try to detach ourselves from our desires and connect ourselves to *avodas Hashem*.

Hashem did the greatest act of love and compassion for us, and planted inside of us a brilliant diamond. Though it can be covered over with all kinds of disgusting waste and excrement, on the inside it is still completely clean and pure. There is a holy place inside of us, which can never be uprooted.

Even if we don't know what we ever did to deserve such a gift from Hashem, and we feel utterly unworthy of having a Jewish soul; nevertheless, it's there inside of us, and we can never remove it.

Therefore, every morning when we say the *berachah* "shelo asani goy," we should be filled with incredible joy. Through no merit of our own, we were blessed to be one of Hashem's beloved children and, like a loving, compassionate Father; He will never give up on us. There is and *always* will be a piece of pure goodness inside of us, and at any moment, even from the lowest physical and spiritual places; we can connect ourselves to that piece of holy G-dliness and remove ourselves from our darkness to become closer to Hashem.

Even if we don't see any external changes, internally we've become greatly transformed.

Nevertheless, it could be that for a long time after we begin to focus on the contrast between us and non-Jews we may not see any change in our ability to overcome our *yetzer harah*. We've spent so long running after the *yetzer harah* that he will not leave us alone so quickly! However, we're not the same as before. If we indulge in our desires, it is not without a fight. Even as we're drinking beer after beer, deep down inside we know this is *not* who we really are. This is *not* what we really want. We're *not* like *goyim* at some fraternity.

If we look at inappropriate images on our phones, we actually hear a voice inside of us telling us to turn it off. We realize that what we're doing is wrong, and underneath it all, we have a strong yearning to be able to stop. We know that this is not what we're here in this world to do. We are so far beyond this. We are holy Jews!

What's changed? Instead of constantly seeing our shortcomings and getting down on ourselves; we begin to focus on the good that's within every one of us, no matter what we've done. Although we may still be very far from reaching our ultimate goals, we have achieved incredible accomplishments through our desire for Hashem and all of the seemingly "little" things that we do for Him.

No matter what we do, we can't mess up the fact that we're a Jew.

Additionally, if we stick with this path and continue to strengthen ourselves with everything that distinguishes us from the *goyim*; without question, we will eventually succeed in transforming ourselves completely. If we don't give up on recognizing the vast differences between us and the other nations, and we try even in the smallest ways to separate ourselves from their physical desires; Hashem will have compassion on us and help us out, like our Sages say (Yuma 38b), "One who comes to purify himself, receives assistance [from Heaven.]"

Slowly but surely, we will be able to attach ourselves even more to our *neshamah* and break ourselves from our physicality. Then, we can see that we really have an incredible desire for Hashem and His mitzvos. We will be able to taste the sweetness of Shabbos. We will be able to relish in the words of *Kiddush* and *Ahavah Rabbah*. We will be able to feel just how precious our learning is to Hashem.

Even if we fall back into our temptations, we know just how to pick ourselves back up: by comparing ourselves to a *goy* and finding the extraordinary beauty of our Jewish *neshamah*.

Chapter Fourteen

The Illness: I am who I am, and there's no way I'll ever be able to change.

We experience this world as incredibly monotonous. Every day is pretty much the same story. The sun comes up and goes down. It's always hot in the summer and cold in the winter. We follow the same halachos day in and day out. We work in the same office with more or less the same people and we do the same things. We learn in the same kollel for the same hours. We always have the same commute.

This is true about our internal reality as well. We have the same worries and fears, day after day, and year after year. We have the same attachment to physical desires. We get frustrated and angry over the exact same things. We get into the same arguments with our friends and family.

It seems like these things are simply part of our "nature." We were just born that way. We are who we are. Life doesn't change, and neither do we. We could take a picture of who we are today, and match it up perfectly to the one from ten years ago. And the older we get, the more the possibility to transform seems more distant, until we forget about it altogether.

The Rebbe's Prescription: You must believe that you have the ability to hit the "erase" button and completely start over at any moment! (Based on Likutei Halachos, Krias HaTorah 6)

Our bar mitzvah is the ultimate proof that all of us have the ability to transform our lives.

Even though it seems like it is impossible for us to break free of the past and make a fresh start, we must believe that each one of us has the ability to do so. The proof is that we've done it before. There was a time when we were twelve years old, when we weren't obligated by the Torah to do mitzvos. We learned in cheder and we played with our friends.

Of course, we observed many mitzvos but we knew that our actions weren't being recorded in Hashem's book. We were just "practicing" the Torah, but yet not actually performing it. It doesn't really matter so much who wins in the pre-season scrimmages.

Then one day, we turned thirteen. All of a sudden, everything changed. We were completely transformed on the inside and out. We bought a whole new wardrobe of adult suits. Maybe we put on a hat for the first time. We began laying tefillin and learning long days in yeshivah. We represented the congregation and had our first aliyah to the Torah.

Everything became real: We were no longer just practicing for the big leagues, we were actually in it!

We were more careful about keeping Shabbos, because now it was really counted. We were more careful about fasting Yom Kippur, because now it really mattered. We were more careful to make sure our candy was kosher, because now we really had to keep ourselves pure.

We also had a new strength and inspiration for learning Torah. We tried to focus harder and take on extra *chavrusahs*. We tried to overcome some of our silly behaviors and act more mature.

It was exciting to go to shul and daven every day with our tefillin on, since we felt like our *tefillos* were really important now. We could now be the tenth man for the minyan. We could now daven for the *amud*, lead the entire *tefillah*, and exempt other adult Jews of their obligations. *Amazing*!

Through our faith in the Torah and the Sages, we can find the inspiration to start over.

When we reflect on this transformation it is truly remarkable. How did we make such drastic changes in our life from one day to the next?

The answer is, of course, that the Torah told us to do so. Our Sages taught us that at thirteen years old, a boy becomes a man in the eyes of the Torah. Since we believe very strongly in our Sages, we spent months preparing ourselves spiritually for the transformation; until when the day finally came, we excitedly rose to the occasion and became a full-fledged member of the tribe, and began our life anew.

From here, we see that each one of us has the incredible power to make a new start. This capability is not on the other side of the sea, nor is it in the distant heavens. It is very, very close to us. We've done it before and we can do it again.

All we need to do is exactly what we did at our bar mitzvah: believe in our Sages. Even though in our eyes, the physical world around us doesn't seem to change, and we don't see that we have any spiritual ability to change; our Sages tell us differently.

Our Sages instituted the following phrase to be said twice every day in the blessing of *Yotzer Ohr*: "And in His goodness, [Hashem] renews the act of creation continually each day." This means that, even though the sun came up and went down yesterday just like today; it wasn't the same at all! Every single moment, Hashem is completely transforming all of Creation. Even though the leaves grow on the trees in the spring and wither in the fall every year; it is never exactly the same. Each time, the Master of the Universe recreates the miracles of life all around us in a new way.

Through science, we now have an ever-deeper understanding of the incredible transformation of the physical world. For example, it seems to us that our skin is the same from day to day. We know that over the course of many years, it changes and becomes more loose and wrinkly; but from one day to the next, it appears like nothing's happening. However, science has shown that within a three-week period, all of the cells of our skin have died and been replaced with new ones. This means that Hashem completely renews our physical form every three weeks!

All the more so is this true in the spiritual realm which is beyond the boundaries of physical mass. As we know, our *neshamah* is a piece of Hashem Himself. So too, just like Hashem recreates the entire world, we also have the unbelievable capacity to change. Every day, we can completely forget about what happened before and make a new start. Even from moment to moment, we can let go of our past and begin again.

Therefore, even though we don't understand how it is possible for such incredible transformations to take place in the world around us, and in ourselves as well, it doesn't matter. Our job is to have pure faith in our Sages that this is the reality.

Reb Nosson explains this idea from the verse in Eichah (3:23): "[Your kindness] is renewed each morning, great is Your faithfulness." From here, Reb Nosson says that even if it is completely beyond our ability to understand the constant change that's happening in the Universe; we must have faith that this is the truth. We must have faith that even after many years of committing the same sin day after day; nevertheless, we have the ability to stop ourselves this very moment and make a new start. We must have faith that our bad "habits" are not set into stone, and that from second to second, we really have the freedom to choose a different path in life.

> **The Source of all Creation is completely unaffected by our sins. By connecting to this place, we can change our ways.**

Additionally, in order to truly let go of the past; we must first understand that no matter what damage we've done, it is always possible to rectify. Reb Nosson explains (Likutei Halachos, Birkas HaShachar 5:46) that although a sin has the ability to destroy countless physical and spiritual worlds; there is a place which cannot be affected even by the most atrocious transgressions. Though we have the ability to mess up all forty-nine gates of *kedushah*, in the fiftieth gate we cannot make a dent. It's a place where evil cannot reach. It's a place which is beyond any *klipos* or *din*. It is a place of complete and pure compassion.

From this place of pure compassion, it is possible for us to start over. By recognizing the incredible love that Hashem has for us by making the Source of all Creation – the fiftieth gate – a place which we can never destroy; we can reconnect to the purity of the Source of our being and start over. From there, we can erase all of the damage we've caused and recreate ourselves anew. We can accept Hashem's deepest compassion for us, and we can have compassion on ourselves and make a new beginning.

Say it out loud!

Once we have strong faith in the tzaddikim who teach us that each moment is a new possibility, we must then tell ourselves – with the deepest sincerity – that nothing ever existed up until this moment in time. We must wipe the slate totally clean and begin again. Much like our bar mitzvah, we must think to ourselves that everything that happened before no longer matters. Today is the very first day of our lives… Then; we should say out loud, "I'm starting over right now! **Right now, mamash!**"

When should we be starting over? Constantly!

We must know that this process of starting over is not something we do once a lifetime on our bar mitzvah. Nor is it something we only do once a year on Yom Kippur, or once a month on Erev Rosh Chodesh, or once a week on Erev Shabbos. Although, as explained by our Sages, these are opportune times for us to start over and we should certainly do our best to take advantage of them; nevertheless we need to make a new start much more frequently than this (see Shivchei HaRan, 6).

Once a day, especially before we go to bed, is a good time for us to clear the slate. We can take some time to review our day, confess our sins to Hashem, and leave this day behind us. Then, we can wake up the next morning and start life anew. We can begin our day as if we just came into this world.

In fact, our Sages tell us that when we sleep our soul ascends to Heaven, our body tastes one sixtieth of death; so that when we wake up our soul returns to our body, it is as if we were born again. Therefore, they prescribed the prayer *"Modeh Ani,"* for us to say as well as the blessings of *"Asher Yatzar"* and *"Elokai, Neshamah..."* so that we could truly live with this reality and thank Hashem for a new chance to serve Him. Thus, by doing a *vidui* and letting go of our past, we can make the best of this golden opportunity for a new beginning.

Sometimes, often starting over even once a day is not enough; rather, we must do it hundreds or even thousands of times a day. Every single time we make a mistake and we find ourselves getting down on ourselves and slipping into self-criticism; we must stop immediately and start over completely.

The *yetzer harah* uses many tactics to get us to sin, but his primary tactic is sadness. He makes us feel bad about who we are and what we did. This pushes us down and greatly weakens our ability to fight him off. Then, in our weakened state, he can come and cause us to do even worse sins. The result of this is that we feel even worse about ourselves and we become even weaker, so then he can come and push us down even further. This is what our Sages describe as, "Sin causes [more] sin." Thus, we see that our main mistake is the depression that we allow ourselves to fall into after we sin, as this is what leads to more serious transgressions.

To understand the nature of this battle with the *yetzer harah*, take the following parable:

We are fighting in an extremely dangerous battle. There are missiles and bullets flying all around us. We're doing our best to dodge them, left and right, and to reach safety. All of a sudden, we fall and scrape our pinky. We see the blood dripping out of it and we start crying, "Oh no, I hurt my pinky. Ouch!" Since we are so occupied with our poor pinky, we fail to see that at that moment our enemy is standing in front of us, with a loaded bazooka aimed at our head. Boom!

So too, when we succumb to the *yetzer harah's* trick of self-criticism, then we don't stand a chance. He's just waiting to finish us off. Therefore, we must constantly take out our special weapon and wipe him out. We must start over time after time.

At the right time, feeling regret is essential to teshuvah. At the wrong time, however, it is detrimental.

Of course, if we're in a situation in which we can do *vidui* on our previous sins before we hit the restart button, this can be very helpful, as mentioned above. If we can take a short period of time and express to Hashem our deepest regret about our transgressions and sincerely ask Him for forgiveness; then it is easier for us to let go of our past and move forward.

When we understand just how precious one thought of teshuvah is to Hashem, and especially, all the more so, when we express our teshuvah in words; we know this is what we must do in order to fix what we've done. Only then, can we erase our mistakes from our mind and start over with a clean slate. Ideally, it is good for us to feel deep remorse. Nevertheless, even if we're unable to open up emotionally,

Hashem still gladly accepts our teshuvah. Just the fact that we're able to tell Him of our desire to change gives Him incredible *nachas*.

However, we are not always in the right physical and spiritual place to do *vidui*. For example, in the middle of the day when we're busy working or learning, it is not a good time for us to stop in our tracks and repent. When we're spending time with our family or friends, it is not a good time to repent. When we're in the process of doing a mitzvah, it is not a good time to repent. Rather, *vidui* must be done when we have some quiet time to ourselves in a solitude place, with no other distractions or obligations pulling at us.

Indeed, even if we have the time and place; it could be that we're not in the right emotional mindset to do *vidui*. If we're already broken and depressed, then doing a confession will not be productive. On the contrary, it could destroy us even more. Or, if our mind is muddy and confused; we won't be able to see our mistakes clearly, and we won't be able to express them to Hashem. The purpose of our *vidui* must be to bring us closer to Hashem. Therefore, it should only come from a positive place of hope for change and transformation. When we're not in a situation to do such a *vidui*, then we should stay away from it altogether.

Rather, in such situations, we must tell our *yetzer harah* that, at the appropriate time, we are going to deal with our mistakes and do *vidui*. However, right now, we are simply going to block them out of our head totally and go on with our day. We are going to shut out the voice of regret and guilt, and strengthen ourselves to be happy.

Right now, we're going to hit the "erase" button and forget about the past. We're going to break ourselves free from our sin and begin anew. Right now, we're going to pretend, with all sincerity, that this moment is the beginning of our life, and what came before doesn't matter at all, just like a convert coming out of the mikveh.

Our *yetzer harah* will do everything he can to weaken our resolve to change.

However, we can be assured that the *yetzer harah* will not leave us alone so easily, especially when we're accustomed to falling into his trap. Shlomo HaMelech calls the *yetzer harah* "the old and foolish king (Koheles, 4:13)" From this description, we can understand exactly how the *yetzer harah* catches us. As soon as we find the courage to move forward and try again to change, we are immediately thwarted with a barrage of thoughts: "You already tried this before. Did it ever work? Do you really think that anything is different this time around? You know who you are, and you know that's who you will always be. Why put yourself through another disappointment? Stop fooling yourself and give up already."

With this, the *yetzer harah* is able to weaken our resolve. We may still try a little bit to make a new path, but, essentially, we don't really believe that we can do it. Our mind is already clouded with doubt about our decision to give it another go. Therefore, he's already won! Now, he can defeat us easily by throwing a simple obstacle in our path, to prevent us from succeeding right away. With this, he then shows us that our cause is futile, and since we're already confused with doubt; this is enough to knock us down completely. Thus, the "old and foolish king" tricks us every time; with the thinking that we are too stuck in our ways and there is no way for us to change. We get stuck in the mud and sink down slowly into his trap even more.

No matter how many times we've already tried, this time is completely new.

Therefore, if we want to succeed, we must believe with hundred percent confidence, that right now is a completely new opportunity, and if we put our minds to it, we can undergo a complete transformation. We must forget about how many times we've tried before and what the previous outcomes were. Even if this is the thousandth time we're starting over already in one day; this time, we have a completely new chance to change. Even if it's the millionth time in our lifetime that we've tried to overcome a specific physical desire or bad *middah*; nevertheless, this time we *can* do it. This time, we can alter the course of history and start a new chapter in our lives.

Not a single attempt is ever lost! Eventually, we will overcome.

Nevertheless, if we are still unsuccessful in our new attempt, we can't get down on ourselves. *We did not fail at all!* Rather, we must believe that all our attempts to change didn't go to waste. Each time that we pick ourselves up and try again; even if we are completely unsuccessful, nevertheless, we continue to build up even more strength against our *yetzer harah*. Each time we fashion new weapons to fight him, and even if his weapons are able to defeat us this time; nevertheless, the next time around we are better armed.

The Zohar HaKadosh says that not a single good desire ever goes to waste (see Terumah 150). All the more so, this is true when we actually try to bring our desire into action. Nothing that happens afterwards can ever take away our precious attempts to do teshuvah, and with time, the accumulation of these attempts will give us the strength to overcome.

We must understand that we are not just fighting a battle with our *yetzer harah*. Rather, it is a war. In a war, one side can lose many battles and they are still not out of it. In fact, if they hold their ground and don't retreat, and they continuously recharge and renew themselves, more often than not, they will win the war.

Therefore, even though to us it seems that we're not making any progress whatsoever in our attempts to start over, and perhaps we're falling even further away from Hashem, we have to be incredibly stubborn in our belief that if we keep trying, the enemy will eventually fall. It's just a matter of time.

We must cherish even the smallest amount of progress, and use it to fight against our *yetzer harah*.

And the moment, we're able to see even the slightest transformation, we must use this as proof that we can succeed. Even the tiniest improvement should give us incredible strength to fight our *yetzer harah*. Every time the voice comes into our head telling us that we're just wasting our time and energy by trying to start over, we can respond by reminding ourselves of the real evidence we have that this is simply not true. Change is possible, even after years and years of sin. We were able to do a little bit, and now we can do a little bit more.

Through this, the ball starts rolling and we become empowered in our life. We are no longer just victims of our desires and slaves to our body. We are no longer slaves to our anger and *kavod*. We're no longer stuck in the same self-destructive habits and sins which run us into the ground time after time. Rather, we're free. We're able to make our own decisions, and choose the path that we want to take. We're able to block out our desire for pizza and stop looking at immodest things on our phone. These things have no control over us anymore. We're able to hold ourselves back from screaming at our wife and children, even when we're being tested to the max.

The war is never over, but now we know how to fight.

Obviously, the war with the *yetzer harah* is never over. Until the day we die, the *yetzer harah* will always test us. However, each time we start over; we're landing a massive upper-cut in his face and knocking him out. Then, after we win the match we often face an even stronger opponent, like our Sages say, "The greater one is, the greater is his *yetzer harah*." But even this new enemy, in the guise of the *yetzer harah* will certainly test us; but he also doesn't stand a chance. Now, we own the tools for battle and we can use them over and over. Indeed, we can change ourselves bit by bit. We can prove that we are holy Jews, who are not bound by our zodiac sign. We are above the constellations and we can choose our own destiny (which is, obviously, preordained by Hashem). We can make a new path in our lives every time we fall. With this, we will never become old until the end of days, and we will constantly become closer to Hashem.

Chapter Fifteen

The Illness: I've made such incredible mistakes that I feel like my avodas Hashem is worthless.

Sometimes, we make big mistakes. We do things that seem so destructive, that we think that there's no way we could really fix them. Maybe, we slept all day and missed *Krias Shema* and *shacharis*. Maybe, we got very arrogant and spoke *lashon harah* about another Jew or we watched something inappropriate on our smartphone. Perhaps, we didn't feel like going to yeshiva, and we went to a bar instead or we became addicted to drugs, pills, or alcohol. It could be we succumbed to our physical desires and transgressed the Torah; may Hashem save us!

Whatever it was, it seems to us like that's it! We think we've fallen so far that it's simply not possible to get back up. We tend to think that from such a low place, how could our *avodas Hashem* be worth anything? We have the feeling that we've messed up *so* badly that even the Torah and mitzvos that we're still able to do are meaningless.

So we continue on with our life like everything is okay on the outside, but deep inside we've completely given up. We're lost. We're stuck and depressed. Then one sin leads to another, and we find ourselves spiraling down a dark path of despair and hopelessness, until we feel sure that there's no way out.

The Rebbe's Prescription: The further you fall away from Hashem, the more important your mitzvos are. (Based on Likutei Halachos, Birkas Hareyach 3)

Adam HaRishon shattered the glass ball of *kedushah* with his sin.

When we find ourselves falling into despair, the most important thing we must know is that our sins are, in fact, incredible opportunities. Although we should never purposely transgress the Torah, when it happens, G-d forbid, we should recognize that now we have a chance to do something truly remarkable. Now, we have a chance to do something that even the greatest tzaddikim could never do. We have a chance to bring Mashiach.

Based on the teachings of the Ari *z"tl*, Reb Noson *z"tl* explains that before the sin of Adam HaRishon, all of the spiritual and physical worlds that Hashem created were whole and complete. There was no brokenness, darkness, or suffering. Everything was "Gan Eden," so to speak. If Adam had listened to Hashem and not eaten from the Tree of Knowledge, this would have achieved the purpose of creation and the world would have never tasted the bitterness of exile from HaKadosh Baruch Hu.

However, when Adam sinned, he broke the perfection of both the physical and spiritual worlds. The result of this was that countless sparks of *kedushah* became distanced from their Source and fell into the contamination of the physical world. Therefore, Adam was expelled from Gan Eden to go and find these sparks in the world in order to lift them back up to their proper place.

It was as if Adam had taken a large glass bowl and smashed it on the ground, causing millions of shards of glass to disperse in all directions. Then, he had to clean up his mess by going around and picking up every single piece, one by one, until he could rebuild the bowl.

The rectification of all sin is by finding the sparks of holiness that are hidden in the physical world.

Because Adam's sin caused such incredible brokenness and destruction, it was not possible for him to finish the job himself. Rather, the responsibility was passed down to his offspring throughout the generations until the coming of Mashiach, to continue picking up these sparks of *kedushah* and return them to the world from which they came.

Every object of this world contains these sparks of *kedushah*, just we cannot see them since they are covered over by physical matter. Due to the concealment of these holy sparks, we have freedom of choice. If we use the physical world for our own desires, we perpetuate the sin of Adam by causing more brokenness and further dispersion of the sparks. However, by attaching ourselves to the *kedushah* in this physical world and extracting it from the physical matter, we rectify the sin of Adam and all the sins of other generations since. This is the purpose of our existence: to redeem these sparks from their contamination, and return them to their Source.

Through every single mitzvah and word of *kedushah*, we fix the brokenness of this world.

We do this by following the laws of the Torah. When we wash our hands in the morning, we purify sparks of *kedushah* in the world of *Asiyah*, removing them from their covering of *tumah*. When we put on our tallis and tefillin, we rectify sparks from the realms of *Yetzirah*, *Beriah*, and *Atzilus*. With each section of davening – berachos, korbanos, etc. – we rectify sparks correlating to specific spiritual worlds.

Every berachah that we make on our food rectifies the sparks that are in that food. Every word of Torah which we say lifts up countless sparks. By being honest in our business, we fix the sparks of *kedushah* in whatever objects we're handling. When we give tzedakah, we rectify the sparks of *kedushah* in the money we make. In short, through every mitzvah we do, we are bringing the world closer to perfection by lifting up the sparks of *kedushah* in the world all around us. Even if we don't understand the teachings of Kabbalah at all, just by simply looking at the countless pages of *kavanos* of the Ari, *z"tl* for one *berachah* or one mitzvah in the Torah, we begin to fathom the depth of rectification we create by doing Hashem's will.

The biggest sparks are lost in the lowest physical places.

But, not all sparks were distributed equally. When the glass bowl was dropped, some pieces fell further from their Source than others. In addition, some pieces were bigger, while others were tiny shards. Some of the sparks in the physical world are closer to *kedushah* and do not need such a profound rectification; while others have fallen *mamash* to the bottom of the dark pit of the physical world. In fact, it is the most exalted sparks that are lost in the lowest places. As explained above, since their light is so great, they must be concealed in the deepest darkness so we won't be able to see them to retain our freedom of choice.

Indeed, it is mainly the sparks hidden in places that are completely void of *kedushah* that Mashiach is waiting for. These sparks that are lost in places where it seems almost impossible to serve Hashem are *the most important* in bringing the ultimate Redemption. So, when is Mashiach going to come already? When some Jew in some desolate place, far, far away from Hashem, does a mitzvah!

When we contemplate these words of the Ari, we see that there is truly never a reason to despair. No matter what disgusting and contaminated physical places we may find ourselves in; it is possible to attach ourselves to Hashem. In fact, it is specifically in those places that it is important for us to keep Torah and mitzvos, in order to lift up the greatest sparks of *kedushah*.

For example, when we're completely surrounded by *goyim* with the tempting smell of non-kosher food wafting through the air, and massive immodest advertisements stretching until the sky – we have to know that no matter the reason that brought us here – right now, we have a chance to lift up wondrous sparks of *kedushah*. How? Simply by saying a *berachah* and taking a drink of a kosher soda. In fact, even by just wearing a *kippah* and tzitzis in such a place can make a huge tikkun; since we're revealing our faith that it is possible to connect to Hashem (and lift up holy sparks) even there.

Another example is when we find ourselves in a place completely removed from the *frum* world, like a small town in the middle of nowhere, or a place far out in nature. Even though such places seem completely void of any connection to the Torah – as there's not a single shul within a hundred miles and perhaps no one has ever davened there before – just by standing there for a few minutes to daven *minchah*, we're able to bring the Redemption closer. Perhaps, the entire purpose of the existence of that place was just for our one *Shemoneh Esrei* prayer.

When we fall into dark spiritual places, we have the greatest opportunity to reveal Hashem's *kedushah*.

Additionally, Reb Nosson explains that a Jew living in such desolate places, like Idaho or Alaska, is generally not so religious. He's so removed from the Torah society that he hardly knows anything about keeping mitzvos. He's completely surrounded by *goyim* and assimilated to their ways. In other words, he's almost completely fallen off the map of *kedushah*.

However, because of his distance, every little thing that he does is that much more important. Specifically in his location dwell the highest sparks of *kedushah*. They are waiting there since the first sin of Adam, just for him to do a mitzvah for Hashem. Through this, he can return them to their Source and bring Mashiach.

Although the simple understanding of the Ari is that this refers to distant physical places; this explanation of Reb Nosson makes it clear that the same is true about distant spiritual places. Therefore, the lower we fall into sin and destruction, the more of an opportunity we have to do something incredible. The further we stray away from

Hashem, the more important it is that we strengthen ourselves to serve Him.

It could be that on the outside it seems as though we're connected to places of *kedushah*; we're living, working and learning in a completely *frum* setting. However, on the inside we find ourselves very far from Hashem. Our neighbors and friends don't realize that anything is wrong; even our family members often don't know. But, we know what we've done and we feel completely broken and hopeless inside.

In these moments it is critical for us not to give up, and to remember that, on the contrary, since we've made such serious mistakes, now we have the opportunity to reveal Hashem in the lowest places and rectify some of the holiest sparks of *kedushah*. We must strengthen ourselves that every little thing that we do for Hashem in such contaminated spiritual places – such as putting on tefillin, saying even a few words of prayer, learning one Mishnah, or even just having a thought of teshuvah – is able to make a much bigger tikkun than even the greatest tzaddik could ever make.

Of course, Hashem loves the tzaddikim, and their *deveikus* in Him through their *avodah* is what inspired Hashem to create the world. Nonetheless, since they're on such exalted levels of *kedushah*, they simply cannot go down and fix the sparks that have fallen to the lowest places. Thus, the main purpose of the true tzaddikim – who are the shepherds of every generation – is to inspire those of us who are very far from Hashem to strengthen our faith that every little thing is of utmost importance to Hashem and all of Creation. We are, so to speak, their messengers to lift up the sparks from all the distant physical and, more importantly, spiritual places.

Therefore, even by just washing our hands and saying a berachah in the morning we are doing something truly remarkable. Even simple halachahs – such as putting on the right shoe before the left and not dressing completely like a *goy* – make an enormous tikkun in the world. Any sincere attempt to break ourselves away from doing a sin is a monumental achievement.

Hashem loves a *ba'al teshuvah* precisely because he's so far away.

This idea is echoed by what our Sages say (Brachos 34b): "In the place where a *ba'al teshuvah* stands, even a complete tzaddik cannot stand." The simple understanding is that a *ba'al teshuvah* is somehow able to reach a higher level than a complete tzaddik. However, this doesn't seem to make sense; since how could the tzaddik be a complete tzaddik if the *ba'al teshuvah* is even higher than him?

Rather, we can understand this through using the literal translation of our Sages. They are showing us that the incredible value of the *ba'al teshuvah* over a pure tzaddik is the fact that he's not on such a high level. On the contrary, he's on such a low level that the tzaddik can't go down and stand in his place. Nonetheless, it is specifically for this reason that the *ba'al teshuvah* is so praiseworthy. From such darkness, every mitzvah he does reveals an incredible light, which is hidden so far away from Hashem, that even the greatest tzaddik cannot reveal it.

Proof that this is our Sages' intention is shown by the following verse: "Peace, peace, to the one who is far away and to the one who is close, said Hashem." From the fact that the verse mentions the "one who is far away" – i.e. the ba'al teshuvah – first, our Sages show that the *ba'al teshuvah* takes precedence over the tzaddik. But, at the end of the day, the verse still calls the *ba'al teshuvah* "far away." This is precisely because he is far away and yet, he's still trying to serve Hashem that Hashem calls out to him first and gives him precedence over the tzaddik. Specifically, when we're very far away from Hashem do we have the opportunity to give Him the greatest *nachas*.

Therefore, if we find our *yetzer harah* telling us that we've already messed up beyond repair and we might as well just throw in the towel, we should never give in. Rather, we should respond that on the contrary, now it is an even more important time for us to work on our *avodas Hashem*. Now is our moment to shine; now we can really make a difference!

And if we still find ourselves falling further, with the *yetzer harah* causing us thoughts of complete and utter despair; we must stay strong and say that our chance to bring Mashiach is now even greater than it was before.

Yisro paved the way for all of us to leave behind our *avodah zarah* and glorify Hashem's name.

The greatest example of this idea in the Torah comes from Yisro: Our Sages explain that before Yisro met Moshe Rabbeinu, not only had he tried every form of idol worship in the world, he had even become a priest in his devout service of *avodah* zarah (see Rashi on Shemos 2:16). He was considered one of the leaders of his generation – along with Amalek and Bilam – in heretical beliefs and practices.

However, when he saw the incredible miracles that Hashem did for the Nation of Yisroel at the splitting of the Yam Suf, and the Divine assistance that the Jews received in the battle with Amalek, he decided to leave it all behind and convert to Judaism (see Shemos 18).

The Zohar HaKadosh explains (Yisro 69a) that at the moment when Yisro recognized the true existence of Hashem and the greatness of His people, Hashem's name was glorified in all the higher and lower worlds. It was precisely because Yisro came from such a low place of devout idol worship, that he was able to lift up the most incredible sparks of *kedushah* and give Hashem the greatest splendor.

From the story of Yisro, we can take incredible *chizuk*. Even if we've committed the most atrocious sins and rebelled against Hashem, G-d forbid. Even if we've fallen deep into the pit of today's idol worship for money. Even if we've become devoutly addicted to pills, drugs, or alcohol, may Hashem save us. Nonetheless, we must recognize that now more than ever, we can give Hashem the greatest *kavod* and rectify the entire Creation. Now more than ever, we can transform the world and help to bring Mashiach.

By simply not giving up and trying to do whatever mitzvah is before us, we can turn everything around. By awakening ourselves to open a *sefer Tehillim* and daven, or to learn even one Mishnah, we can lift up the greatest sparks of *kedushah* and reveal to the entire universe that all forms of *avodah zarah* are completely empty and meaningless. Through this, we can accomplish the entire purpose of creation: to bring awareness of Hashem to the world.

Through strengthening ourselves with this idea, we see that we can really fix our mistakes. We can really start over and lift ourselves up. From here, we can find the faith to believe that just like we have the ability to mess up, so too, we have the ability to fix. Indeed, after a while, we will be able to pull ourselves completely out of our sins and do complete teshuvah.

Chizuk in Connecting to Tzaddikim

Chapter Sixteen

The Illness: I would like to purify myself and serve Hashem like a tzaddik; but every time I try, it feels like Hashem is pushing me further away.

Sometimes, we have dreams of what it would be like to be a tzaddik. We imagine the incredible feeling of constant attachment to the Master of the Universe. We think about having complete control over our thoughts and having no desires at all for this World. We picture tasting the sweetness of davening with perfect *kavanah* and learning Torah all day and night.

With this, we get inspired to lift ourselves out of the trash and become closer to Hashem. We try to overcome our animalistic desires and put our mind through the car wash. We try to devote ourselves to our *avodas Hashem* in a deeper way.

However, we're often met with an unbelievable negative counterforce which pushes us exactly in the opposite direction. It seems that every time we try to take one step forward, we get knocked ten steps back. Right after we come out of the car wash, we run into an even deeper pool of muck.

So, *we give up!* We think that tzaddikim must have been born with such holy *neshamos* that they didn't have to go through any of this. They came from families with impeccable *yichus* and grew up in extraordinarily pure environments. Of course they also worked hard to reach their exalted levels, but they didn't have to go through the difficult challenges that we're faced with.

To us, it seems like we will never climb out of our garbage dump; let alone achieve a level of true *deveikus* in Hashem.

The Rebbe's Prescription: The main difference between a tzaddik and an average Jew is that a tzaddik never gives up. (Based on Likutei Mohoran II, 48)

The greatness of a tzaddik is not due to his *yichus*, rather the stubbornness of his *ratzon* for Hashem.

Although, it may seem to us like our tzaddikim were born with the "DNA" which allowed them the natural ability to achieve high spiritual levels without struggling with their physical desires and bad *middos*; Rebbe Nachman teaches us that this is simply *not* true. Every single Jew must go through trials and tribulations before he can come close to Hashem. Every Jew goes through incredible struggles with their lusts and physical desires. Just as each person must work on overcoming his obsession for wealth, his animalistic passions for food, his need for *kavod* and recognition, and toil to develop true humility.

No one is simply born on such a level that they don't have to be tested. No matter how great someone's ancestors were and no matter how inspiring their own *chinuch* was; they still have a *yetzer harah* and the freedom to choose to do right or wrong. Each one of us was given a holy Jewish *neshamah* taken directly from Hashem's throne of glory, and cast down into the physical darkness of this world. Each one of us has a piece of Hashem Himself inside of us, even though sometimes we may act like an animal on the outside.

So, what is the exact difference between our tzaddikim and us? The answer is simple: our tzaddikim never give up. Our tzaddikim never despair and never stop trying to overcome their obstacles. Our tzaddikim never let go of their *ratzon*. Through their unbelievable stubbornness to succeed, they are able to rise above all of their difficulties and reach lofty heights in *avodas Hashem*.

Rebbe Nachman shares with us his own life's struggles, in order for us to understand how he was able to succeed.

Rebbe Nachman explains this to us by sharing his own life story with us, in the *sefer* Shivchei HaRan. He was born into one of the holiest families of Klal Yisroel. He was a great-grandson of the Baal Shem Tov z"tl, who was himself a descendent of Dovid HaMelech, may he rest in peace. He was named after his grandfather, Reb Nachman Haradenker, one of the primary *talmidim* of the Baal Shem Tov, and it is well-known (as told by numerous first-hand witnesses) that both his mother, Faiga, and grandmother, Odle, had high levels of *ruach hakodesh*.

Nevertheless, Rebbe Nachman describes in detail the multitude of trials and tribulations he had to overcome when he was young. He describes how heavy *avodas Hashem* was for him, and the unbelievable effort he had to exert to achieve anything in *kedushah*. For example, he struggled greatly with his learning. It was very hard for him to understand the Talmud, so he studied Mishnayos. But even then, he had difficulty… So, he cried out to Hashem in prayer until he was able to understand his Mishnayos! Then, he did the same for the Talmud and other *sefarim*; he had to put in an incredible amount of effort just to understand the basic *p'shat*.

He tells of all the countless ups and downs that he went through… For example, he would make up his mind to make a new start in *avodas Hashem* and he would daven with *kavanah* and learn consistently for a few days. But then, he would fall away from his *avodah* for a while, until he would pick himself up and make another attempt. This happened over and over again countless times; until one day, he made up his mind to hold his ground and not fall away from Hashem.

Rebbe Nachman says that it seemed to him like Hashem was pushing him away. Even after years of trying to come closer to Him, he still hadn't changed at all. Sometimes, he would even question Hashem's ways and feel bitter about his lack of success. But then, he would remind himself that Hashem only acts with compassion, and he wouldn't give up.

He went through a number of incredible tests with lust, in which he had the opportunity to fulfill his desire and almost gave in… But instead, he screamed and called out to Hashem for help and was able to escape. He went through countless battles until after an unbelievable amount of effort; he was able to break through completely.

Then, he had to work extremely hard to overcome his desire for food. It seemed to him that he could break all his other desires, but this desire, he simply couldn't manage to overcome and it would have to remain that way… Nevertheless, he didn't give up until he was able to overcome his desire for food as well.

The same was true with the *middos* of Rebbe Nachman. At first, he was easy to anger and was very strict with other people. However, he realized that this was not the will of Hashem, so he worked hard to overcome his anger.

At the end of "Shivchei HaRan," Reb Nosson z"tl writes that even though it is disgraceful to mention all the struggles that Rebbe Nachman went through – since he later reached such exalted levels in *kedushah* and *avodas Hashem* that none of us can begin to fathom – nevertheless, Rebbe Nachman wanted to make these stories public, in order for us to understand where he started out and the incredible amount of effort he had to make until he became a true tzaddik. Rebbe Nachman says that we shouldn't think even for a second that it was due to his *yichus* that he achieved such high levels. Rather, he worked very hard and never gave up. Throughout all of his tribulations, he cried countless tears and davened myriads of prayers until he was able to succeed. He constantly poured out his heart over the verses of *Tehillim* and other *tefillos*. He strengthened his *ratzon* for Hashem time after time. Nothing came easy to him, but he kept on trying…

When we see the end result, it is very hard for us to believe. When we see how he managed to completely rid himself of any physical desire, reach the highest levels in *avodas Hashem* and *deveikus* in the *Or HaEin Sof*, and bring down the unbelievable *chiddushei HaTorah* – which have the ability to help every Jew do teshuvah and bring the Final Redemption – it seems impossible that he went through anything that even resembles our life's struggles. But he did!

Despite the seemingly impossible challenges with which we are faced, we must never despair!

From the life of Rebbe Nachman, we must take incredible *chizuk*. We are all struggling to *serve*.

Hashem; we have barely any desire to daven. Many of us can hardly sit for more than a few minutes over a Gemara before we start to bug out and have to check our smart phone. For many of us, it is almost impossible to give away our hard-earned money to tzedakah.

Sometimes, we get lost in the *goyishe* world of physical temptation and we commit sin after sin. We feel completely broken and disconnected from Hashem. We feel swallowed up by darkness.

Not only that, but whenever we try to pick ourselves up and do teshuvah, we are met with such unbelievable challenges that it seems impossible for us to succeed. Every effort we make to change is met with such incredible counterforce that we completely lose hope. The test is just too great for us to overcome.

We think that, perhaps, if we had been born into a family of *ovdei Hashem*, then we might have a chance… Perhaps, if we had parents and rabbonim who had given us the right support and good *chinuch*, then we might have chance. Maybe, if we had made the right decisions when we were younger, then we might have chance.

But, with the spiritual tools that we were given and all the mistakes we've already made; it appears as if there is simply no way for us to transform our ways and reach higher levels in *avodas Hashem*.

But, Rebbe Nachman says, "There is no [reason to] despair in the world!" We have to be strong. We have to hold our ground. We have to keep trying. We have to believe that we have the ability to overcome the physical and spiritual obstacles that are before us. We have to believe that we can get out of our darkness and do teshuvah.

We must remember that each and every tzaddik went through similar challenges. They were all faced with incredible tests. They too, had the feeling that Hashem was pushing them away and it seemed to them that they just didn't have the ability to succeed. But they didn't give up, and they merited to amazing *deveikus* in Hashem and His mitzvos.

So too, we must learn from their experiences. We must recognize that we have no idea what our true potential really is. We have no idea just how far we can go in *avodas Hashem*. Our destiny is completely in our hands.

Therefore, whatever happened in the past doesn't matter at all! Right now, we can strengthen ourselves and start over. Right now, we can decide definitively that we will never give up; no matter what obstacles we are faced with and no matter how far away we feel from Hashem. Right now, we can attach ourselves to our *ratzon* for Hashem and be incredibly stubborn in the face of all of our struggles.

We have the ability to bring out the tzaddik that is already within us, as the verse says, "And your nation (Yisroel) are all tzaddikim." From here, we see the true potential embedded in our souls to withstand and overcome even the most impossible challenges.

Prayer is our greatest weapon to defeat our *yetzer harah*.

So how do we do it? In addition to having a stubborn *ratzon* to succeed, we must follow Rebbe Nachman's example and use our greatest weapon: tefillah. We must express our yearning for Hashem in words. We must beg and plead with Hashem to help us. We must entreat Him to get us out of our physical desires and give us the strength and focus to learn and daven. We must scream to Hashem to give us the courage to keep going. We must cry our eyes out to Him to help us hold our ground and not despair.

Indeed, if we are stubborn enough with our *ratzon* and our tefillos, we will eventually succeed; just like all the tzaddikim who give testimony that this is the only way to overcome obstacles in *avodas Hashem*.

Even if we lose round after round, with one good blow we can be victorious.

Additionally, we must understand that the harder we try to succeed in coming closer to Hashem, the more opposition we will face – that is the nature of our existence. The entire World was created just for us to have freedom of choice, so there will always be a fair fight between us and our *yetzer harah*. Therefore, every time we give him a blow and try to daven with the deepest *kavanah*; we have to know that our *yetzer harah* is going to launch a counter attack of distracting thoughts and confusion on us. Nevertheless each time, we must strengthen ourselves more and more to overcome him.

Even if we're getting knocked around and are losing round after round of the match, that we are going day after day without being able to daven even one *Shemoneh Esrei* with *kavanah*; we must listen to the advice of our boxing coach – Rebbe Nachman – and stay in the game. We must understand that even if we lost the first fifteen rounds, with one good punch – one inspired tefillah – we can destroy our *yetzer harah* and win the entire match! Then, all of our previous tefillos will go straight up to Heaven (see Likutei Mohoran I, 99).

Just when we think we've fallen, we've actually achieved a higher level.

After we manage to succeed in davening with *kavanah* or reaching the next level in *avodas Hashem*; very often it seems like we fall back to square one. We, once again, find ourselves struggling with the same challenges as before and it appears to us like we lost any progress that we thought we had made.

Despite this, Rebbe Nachman reveals to us that, in truth, we haven't fallen at all. Rather, since we have risen to a new level in our *avodah*; there's a new enemy who is even stronger and bigger than before, who's trying to stop us from serving Hashem. Thus, it appears like we are much weaker than we really are. Nonetheless, with time and a stubborn *ratzon*, we will be able to defeat him as well (see Likutei Mohoran I, 25).

Giving up is not an escape.

Although, the struggle to continue fighting may be very difficult and the temptation to despair and give in to our *yetzer harah* may seem extremely appealing; this only causes us greater suffering. When we let go and surrender to this, a dark bitterness enters inside our mind and soul. Our life becomes utterly unbearable and becomes "black with depression." In short, we die on the inside. This is not an option!

Rather, we must hold on to our belief that Hashem wants us to be close to Him. He cherishes our *ratzon* to serve Him and every effort we make is precious to Him; and with time, we will be victorious. Therefore, we must never give up!

Just one more push…

Additionally, we must know that when we come very close to breaking through the wall of obstacles – when it is the very last moment before our *yetzer harah* falls – he will do everything possible to knock us down. He will put all of his strength into his one last effort to prevent us from succeeding.

This can be very disheartening. After trying for so long to overcome the *yetzer harah*, it now seems to us like things are only getting much worse! All of a sudden, it appears to us that we've fallen further away from our goal than ever before. Indeed, even when being a hair's breadth away from success; many of us concede to our *yetzer harah* at this point, and fall into his trap. He is able to weaken our *ratzon*, and we fall into the dark pit of despair.

Therefore, we must not be fooled! We must never give up. We must have hope. We must believe that it is only because we're so close to the finish line; that is why the obstacles are so great. We must believe that we have the ability to hold on to our desire and overcome this final test. Regardless of what we're going through, we must close our eyes, and say, "All I want is You, Hashem, all I want is You!"

Then, after days, months, or maybe years have passed, we will look back at our beginnings and be amazed by the strength of the tzaddik inside of us. We will see how the incredible potential within us has come to fruition.

Chapter Seventeen

The Illness: I feel like I'm all alone in my suffering, and there's no one who knows how to help me.

We all go through difficult times. For many of us, most of our life is full of suffering. We are constantly being faced with adversity and we're simply not up for it. We feel too physically and spiritually weak to deal with our problems and try to overcome them. We are under the weather and we need someone to heal us and give us strength.

We look for support from our family and friends. We go to our local Rebbe. We try talking to a therapist. If our issues are not really so severe, then it could be that one of these people may be able to help us. If we're only a little sick, they may have the remedy to treat our symptoms.

However, when we're really lost and broken, and we feel extremely spiritually ill; their advice is not able to comfort us. No matter what they say, they are not able to alleviate our suffering. They do their best to listen and understand us; but at the end of the day, they don't really know how to heal our soul.

So we feel completely hopeless and alone, with no one to help us. We've tried all our resources to remedy our spiritual health, but nothing has worked out.

The Rebbe's Prescription: In each generation there is a great tzaddik who can diagnose and heal all illnesses. Search for him! (Based on Likutei Moharan I, 30)

If we would be very sick, G-d forbid, we wouldn't settle for anything but the best doctor.

When we are overall very healthy, but we come down with a cold, or flu, or any other mild illness, then we go to a family doctor to help us get better. A family doctor is well-trained to diagnose and treat these types of problems. Or perhaps, we don't even go to a doctor at all and we just try to take care of ourselves until the symptoms go away.

However, if G-d forbid, we get a serious illness like a tumor, heart attack, or brain damage, then we wouldn't just go to our regular doctor. We might meet with him to ask him to refer us to the specialist that he recommends; but we wouldn't ever imagine having him treat us by himself. That's not his job; he's not trained to deal with these types of things. Any good family doctor would never try to heal patients with illnesses that are beyond his area of expertise.

Rather, since our life is no joke and we want to do everything we can to survive; we would look for the top doctor in the entire field. We would search through all of the channels available to us in order to find the absolute best. We would spend however much money it would cost to go to a private specialist at the most esteemed hospital. We would even travel very long distances by plane to see this specialist. Our health is the most important thing in the world; so nothing would stop us from getting the absolute best care possible.

When it comes to our spiritual health, we must also do everything possible to get the best care.

If this is true about our physical health, shouldn't it also be true about our spiritual health?! After all, as important as our bodies are to be a vehicle for us to do mitzvos in this world, at the end of the day, they are only a means to an end. Our ultimate goal is the Next World. Of course, we must try to keep our body healthy so that we have the ability to learn as much Torah and do as many mitzvos as possible. However, our main focus is on the Torah and mitzvos themselves. Our sole purpose in This World is to serve Hashem as best we can.

Therefore, even if we are as physically healthy as a marathon runner or bodybuilder; but we are struggling greatly in our *avodas Hashem*, we're actually extremely sick and in serious spiritual danger. If we're lost in the desires of this world – money, *kavod*, elicit relations, etc. – then we are missing the entire purpose of our existence on earth. If we're constantly attached to bad *middos* such as anger, arrogance, laziness, and depression; our *neshamah* is literally screaming out in agony and pain. If we can't sit down to learn for more than a couple minutes without checking our smart phone, and we've given up on davening with *kavanah*, our soul is dying of thirst and starvation.

Many of us have fallen so far that the arteries of our heart are clogged with the filth of physical temptation. We have a huge tumor in our stomach from excessive eating and drinking. We have massive brain damage from our heretical thoughts and questions against Hashem. Our life in the Next World is mamash hanging on by a thread.

In such a dire situation, how could we even think of going to a regular doctor? Or perhaps, even going to a therapist or a local Rebbe for help? They may be on a much higher spiritual level than us, and they may be able to help people with less severe spiritual problems; but we need expert treatment. We need the top specialist, since he is the only one who has the remedy to heal our soul. We need a tzaddik who understands the human condition so well, that he is able to diagnose our illness and give us the appropriate advice. We need a tzaddik who knows exactly what we're going through and has a massive warehouse full of medicine just for us.

Only the tzaddik who's at the top of the mountain has the ability to show us the way up.

To understand this idea further, let us take the following parable:

We are trying to climb a mountain to acquire the ultimate treasure; but we can't find the path. We search here and there, with no luck. We are stuck and need help. So, we look to see if anyone else has succeeded in climbing up further than us. A little way up the mountain, we see another person. Since he's been able to reach a much higher place than we have; it seems that for sure he could help us find the correct path. So, we call him on his cell phone.

He tries to help us, but he is unable. He didn't start out in the exact same place as us. Perhaps, he even began his journey from the opposite side of the mountain. In addition, since he hasn't reached the top of the mountain, his view is obstructed by trees; so he can't see so clearly where we need to go.

Then, we lift our eyes up even further, and at the top of the mountain; we see another person. Certainly, he will be able to help us. He can see in all four directions with absolute clear vision. No matter where we're coming from; he can tell us exactly how to find our path. There are no trees or any other obstructions, which will prevent him from figuring out how to help us.

So too, when we begin our journey to reach the ultimate treasure which awaits us in the Next World, but we get stuck in one place – without guidance as to where to go next – we shouldn't think that it's best for us to connect to a Rebbe who is just on a slightly higher level than us; because he'll be able to relate to us and have good advice for our unique situation. We shouldn't think that it'll be best to go to this Rebbe who is only slightly above us; because we could be like him. These are good intentions, but they are misguided; because such a Rebbe won't necessarily have the vision to be able to help us (as shown in the parable).

Rather, we must search for the tzaddik who is at the top of the mountain. Only such a tzaddik who has reached the highest level, through his mesiras nefesh in *avodas Hashem* can help us. Only a tzaddik who has completely broken through his physical desires, will be able to have the clarity to understand what we're going through and know exactly how to help us. Only he has the ability to guide each one of us on our own unique path in becoming closer to Hashem.

Although it seems counter-intuitive; the reality is that the higher the tzaddik is, the lower he can reach. In that, the more he can relate to us and give us the advice we need. Hashem Himself is a prime example of this. It is only because Hashem is so great and exalted in all the Higher Worlds; that He has the ability to come down into the darkest physical realm of This World and fill it with His Presence.

Indeed, if we look honestly at where we're holding, and we try to understand what's going to happen after we leave This World in the the blink of an eye; we should be expending our every effort to find such a tzaddik. Once we find him; we should be spending every single dollar we have to travel to him. We should spend every breath that we have crying out to Hashem, to help us get close to such a tzaddik. We should use all our strength to scream out to Hashem, for the medicine of the tzaddik, which can save our soul from destruction.

We should be looking at every *sefer* available to us, in order to find such a tzaddik. We should be always asking other people if they've found a tzaddik who has helped them with such sicknesses, like ours. We should be yearning for such a tzaddik from the depths of our heart, and be davening to Hashem, without respite, to help us reach the tzaddik who can heal us.

To begin with, we must believe that there is a tzaddik in every generation who is able to bring us back to life; even from our deathbed.

So, why don't we do this? Why are we *so* far away from searching for a tzaddik, that we actually question the legitimacy of many such tzaddikim?

The answer is that we don't really believe that such a tzaddik really exists. We know just how far we've fallen; so we can't fathom that there could be anyone – no matter how great he is – who could know exactly how to help us. We think we are beyond repair. We think we are already on our spiritual deathbed and that it would take a miracle to save us; but we don't believe in such miracles!

Additionally, we have already tried going to many people for help. We've reached out to those whom we thought had the skills to treat us, but to no avail. We thought that since they were so much greater than us and so much closer to Hashem; they must certainly have the medicine to heal us. But it didn't work, and we lost hope.

But, as mentioned before, we were looking in the wrong section of the yellow pages! Instead of looking under the listings for "family doctor," we should have been looking under the listings for "heart surgeon," or "brain tumor specialist." Instead of looking for a Rebbe who is on a higher level than us; we should be looking for tzaddik who is *extremely* close to Hashem, and who has the expertise to help patients who are on their last breath.

We must believe that such a tzaddik exists in every single generation. Our Sages say (Chagiga 3), "There is no orphaned generation [without a tzaddik to lead them]." They also say (Yuma 38) that even before the tzaddik of a previous generation passes away; the tzaddik who will guide the next generation is already born.

From here, we see that there *must* be someone in our generation who can heal us. Hashem doesn't expect us to recover from a terminal illness, without any assistance. He wouldn't leave us like sheep who have gone completely astray, without giving us a shepherd to call us back. In every single generation there has to be a tzaddik who has the ability to guide Klal Yisroel; not only in halachic matters, but rather in deeper spiritual issues as well.

> **From the birth of the Jewish people until today; there has been a tzaddik in every generation who has known exactly how to heal his people.**

This has been true since the beginning of our existence, and it is *still* true today. When we first became a nation upon leaving Egypt; it was only through the guidance of Moshe Rabbeinu that we were able to escape. Since we had fallen into the lowest spiritual depths, only Moshe Rabbeinu – the greatest prophet and leader of the Jewish people in all of history – was able to help us. Since we were so lost in the contamination of Egypt; only a tzaddik like Moshe Rabbeinu, who had reached the highest levels of *deveikus* in Hashem, was able to save our souls from complete destruction. Afterwards, it was only due to Moshe Rabbeinu's exalted level of *kedushah* and his incredible prophetic powers, that we were able to receive the Torah at Har Sinai.

However, this didn't stop with Moshe Rabbeinu… Immediately after Hashem informed Moshe that he would soon die Moshe responded by telling Hashem that He had to appoint someone to guide *klal Yisroel* in his place (see Bamidbar 27:15). The Torah describes the nature of such a leader as someone "who understands the soul of each and every Jew (verse 18, based on Rashi's commentary)." This means that the shepherd of Yisroel must be able to comprehend exactly what each person is going through – all of their struggles and ups and downs – and know precisely what advice each person needs to be spiritually healthy.

Hashem told Moshe to appoint Yehoshua as his successor. So, Moshe placed his hands upon Yehoshua's head and transmitted his amazing spiritual light and leadership capabilities over to him.

But, it didn't end there… The first Mishnah in Pirkei Avos describes how the Torah tradition and the leadership of the Jewish people was passed down from generation to generation; beginning with Moshe Rabbeinu at Har Sinai, and finishing with the Tanaim who lived close to the end of the second Beis HaMikdash. These Tanaim were followed by the Amoraim. The Amoraim were followed by the Geonim. The Geonim were followed by the Rishonim, and the Rishonim by the Acharonim, until this very day.

Although, there was never another prophet like Moshe Rabbeinu, and with each proceeding generation the spiritual level of the tzaddikim declined; nevertheless, all true leaders of *klal Yisroel* received an aspect of *ruach hakodesh*, which allowed them to guide their people as a whole, as well as each specific individual.

Additionally, Rashi explains in parashas Shoftim (Devarim 17:9), that we must follow the "shofet" – leader – of **our days**. This means that, as great as Moshe Rabbeinu was; it is not enough just to learn the Chumash which he wrote. Without the Mishnah and the Talmud, we would have no idea how to perform Hashem's mitzvos. To go even further, without the Shulchan Aruch and modern day *poskim*; we still wouldn't have any clue how to fulfill the Torah. So, we see that we are always in need of the leaders of Klal Yisroel even in our generation, and are obligated to connect ourselves to their teachings.

As mentioned before, this is not only true regarding guidance in halachic matters; rather it is also true about the health of our soul and our relationship to Hashem. In every generation, there has to be a tzaddik who received this spark of *ruach hakodesh* and is able to heal our unique illnesses. It is not enough for us to connect to the tzaddikim of previous times; since their purpose was to help the people of their generation. Nowadays, just like we have new halachic questions; we also have new and more serious spiritual illnesses. Therefore, we must believe that there is also a tzaddik in our generation, who can help us and we are obligated to search for him, in order to receive treatment for our soul.

The biggest obstacle to finding the tzaddik is *machlokes*.

However, even once we believe that such a tzaddik exists and we have a *ratzon* to search for him; there is another obstacle that prevents us from actually doing so: *machlokes* – dissension. The Sages say at the end of Masechtas Sotah that before Mashiach comes, there will be incredible *machlokes* between the tzaddikim. The followers of one tzaddik will say that they have the ultimate truth, while the followers of another tzaddik will say that they have the ultimate truth.

This dissension between the tzaddikim is a powerful weapon which the Other Side (the forces of evil) uses to stop the Redemption. If there was a clear indication exactly who is the tzaddik of our generation, who is the main carrier of the spark of *ruach hakodesh* of Moshe Rabbeinu; then all of us would instantly connect to him, and from his teachings, we would all do complete teshuvah and bring Mashiach immediately. However, in order to prevent this from happening, the Other Side creates incredible confusion and *machlokes* between the tzaddikim. This causes us to lose all hope. *What can we possibly do?* This tzaddik tells us to go one way, and the other tells us to go in the exact opposite direction. Who are we to decide which one to follow?

Our Sages call this dissension the "birth pains" of Mashiach, because it causes great suffering. Since we don't have the ability to decipher which one is right; we don't connect to any of them. Because of machlokes, we throw out advice from all tzaddikim. We don't try to learn their *sefarim* and follow their guidance. We don't go to them to see if they can help us. Some of us don't even believe that they are true tzaddikim at all, and we make fun of them privately and sometimes, even publicly.

Thus, without the spiritual guidance that we need, we are left to our own devices; and we fall very far away from Hashem. We get terminally ill and we suffer greatly. All this is caused by the bitterness of *machlokes*.

We must completely ignore *machlokes* and believe that all the tzaddikim are true (see Likutei Mohoran I, 5:4 and 56:9).

What can we do? It is not in our hands to prevent *machlokes*; since it is a product of the "birth pains" of Mashiach, which are way beyond our control to stop. However, it is in our hands to decide whether we want to pay attention to *machlokes* or not. We don't have to get involved in it at all. We don't have to read about it online, in newspapers, magazines, or other publications. Especially, we don't have to talk about it with others and we can run away from those who speak about it incessantly. If our particular shul gets very involved in *machlokes* and it builds up more and more; then, perhaps, we should find another one.

Then, once we're able to block out the roar of *machlokes* from our head; the next thing we must do is strengthen our faith that, despite the *machlokes*, all of the tzaddikim are true. *We must hold of all of them!* We shouldn't try to figure out who's right and who's wrong, because they're *all* right! Any tzaddik who is able to teach Jews how to live according to the Torah (as passed down through our Sages) is, certainly, on the right path and should never be considered "wrong" in his beliefs.

Even though this is an obvious truth; it is impossible for us to understand it. At the end of the day, one tzaddik tells us to go right and the other tells us to go left. *How can they both be correct?* This concept is what our Sages describe as (Eiruvin 13), "Their [words], and their [words], are the words of the Living G-d – *Elu ve'elu, divrei Elokim Chaim.*"

A classic example of this is the *machlokes* between Beis Shamai and Beis Hillel. It is a terrible mistake to say that either of them were wrong, G-d forbid. Even though they disagree on how to expound upon the verses of the Torah, which results in huge practical differences in halachah; nevertheless, they're both right. This is beyond all logic; so we must simply accept it on faith.

So too, we must have the same approach to the leaders of our generation. We must believe that they are all true tzaddikim. And when we perceive *machlokes* between them; we must strengthen our faith that they are all correct in their teachings.

There has to be one tzaddik who has the highest truth.

Nevertheless, just like in the *machlokes* between Beis Shamai and Beis Hillel; it is not possible to try to follow all of the tzaddikim equally, since we can't go left and right at the exact same time. At the end of the day, our Sages chose the halachah to follow Beis Hillel. Thus, even though Beis Shamai is also right; Beis Hillel has a higher level of truth, so to speak.

This can also be understood by the *machlokes* between Yosef HaTzaddik and his brothers. It is known that *all* the sons of Yaakov Avinu were very righteous. Nevertheless, Yosef was on a higher level than all of them and he was fitting to lead them all. However, even though the other brothers were great tzaddikim in their own right; they weren't able to recognize the greatness of Yosef, so they argued with him and, eventually, sold him into slavery. Our Sages say that this caused the Jews to be exiled to Egypt.

Even nowadays, tzaddikim who are the true leaders of *klal Yisroel* exist. Also in our times; there are tzaddikim who, like Yosef, Moshe, and Yehoshua, know how to help each of us come closer to Hashem. However, just like with the sons of Yaakov; it is the argument between the tzaddikim, which is exacerbating the exile of the Jewish people and our own personal exile as well.

Therefore, we must block out the *machlokes* from our head and hold of all the tzaddikim; but at the same time we must realize that not all of them are equally able to help us. No two tzaddikim can be on the exact same level; it is not humanly possible. Even though they are all righteous, one has to be on a higher level than the others; just like the top specialist doctor is in a league of his own, compared to all the other well-trained doctors.

We must search for the true tzaddik with everything we've got.

So, without denouncing any of the tzaddikim; we must search for the one tzaddik of our generation who can truly heal our souls. We must do everything possible to find the one that is right for us. We must look through all the available channels to find the tzaddik who has the remedy for our specific illness. We must be willing to crawl on our hands and knees to reach the tzaddik who can save us from our sins, and bring us to the Next World. We must be willing to disregard any ridicule that we may receive for connecting to such a tzaddik. *We must look for the highest truth, at all costs.*

But, how do we know who is the one? From our perspective, we can't tell the difference between any of the tzaddikim; since they're all on exponentially higher levels than we are. All of the tzaddikim are incredible *talmidei chachamim*: They are all able to daven with the purest *kavanah* and *deveikus*. They are all *kadosh* and separated from the desires of this world. So, it seems like there is no way for us to distinguish between them...

The telling sign of a great tzaddik is one who can help us do teshuvah.

Nevertheless, there actually is an extremely simple way to know which tzaddik to follow: Whomever is able to help us to achieve *yishuv hadaas* and do teshuvah.

The Torah from a particular tzaddik could be incredibly impressive. It could give us deep understandings in the teachings of the Talmud, Shulchan Aruch, and the *poskim*. It could give us wondrous explanations and illuminations of the teachings of the Zohar, Ari z"tl, and books of Chassidus. It could be very inspirational to hear the tzaddik give over Torah and to watch him learn and daven with the utmost *deveikus* in the Creator. To us, it could seem that he is on such an exalted level in *avodas Hashem* that he is, for sure, the one we should attach ourselves to.

However, if we find that his teachings aren't able to awaken our heart to serve Hashem; then he's not the tzaddik for us. If we find that, despite his greatness, he's not able to reach us on our level and help us with our everyday spiritual problems; then he's not the tzaddik for us. If we find that, as lofty as his Torah is, it is not showing us a clear path as to how to connect ourselves to *avodas Hashem* to the best of our ability; then he's not the tzaddik for us.

Rather, the tzaddik we're looking for is the one whose succinct advice is exactly what we need to hear to rise up from our darkness and attach ourselves to Hashem: Whoever can teach us how to daven with incredible inspiration and focus, and help us overcome all of our foreign thoughts. Whoever can teach us how to love learning Torah *so much*, that we don't waste a moment in which we could have opened a *sefer*. Whoever can teach us the unbelievable value of every single mitzvah, and awaken our heart to perform Hashem's commandments with love and awe. Whoever can give us the motivation to get out of bed in the early morning, to serve Hashem and praise Him with all our souls.

Whoever has the ability to save us from running after our desires to make excessive amounts of money; and can implant deep in our minds a constant awareness of the Next World. Whoever has the ability to break us free of our love of *kavod*, and can bring us to true humility and sincerity in everything we do. Whoever can inspire us to close our eyes from seeing immodest images on the street and on our phones; and can give us the strength to overcome the most challenging physical desires.

Whoever has the ability to lift us up when we fall and save us from complete spiritual destruction. Whoever has the ability to make us feel close to Hashem at all times; even if we've done the most grievous sins. Whoever has the ability to heal our broken souls and give us amazing courage in the face of our suffering. Whoever has the ability to arouse within us a deep yearning for Hashem and nothing else. Whoever has the ability to make us *truly* happy; despite everything we're going through physically and spiritually.

And especially; whoever can help us to clear our heads, and come to true *yishuv hadaas*.

A true tzaddik is able to bring us to a higher awareness of Hashem (see Likutei Mohoran II, 8:8).

Although there are many different types of spiritual illnesses; nevertheless, all of them can be attributed to a brain disorder. Our mind is the king of our body; it directs the entire show. Every movement we make originates in our mind; every word we speak originates in our mind. Every mitzvah or *aveirah* that we do is the result of a command from our head. As our Sages say (Sotah 3), "A person only sins if a spirit of craziness enters [his mind]."

And let's face it, we're all pretty crazy! Each of us may have a different mental disorder that causes us to do different sins; since the reality is that we've *all* got some loose screws in our heads. Most of us are missing many screws altogether!

Therefore, a true tzaddik is someone who can help us to achieve *yishuv hadaas*. A true tzaddik is able to teach us how to overcome our worries about the future, and our guilt about the past. He's able to inspire us to block out all of our lustful thoughts and our desires for food, money, and *kavod*. He's able to strengthen us to not be afraid of the weather, our boss, our mortgage, or anything else, but Hashem.

Once our thoughts are free of confusion and desire, the good king – our *daas* – can resume his throne, so to speak, and we can easily do teshuvah. When we're able to control our mind, we can choose exactly what we want to do, and we can stop ourselves from falling into sin. We can attach ourselves to *avodas Hashem* with love and awe and bring out the tzaddik that is within us.

With a clear mind, we are able sit and learn for hours at a time; even without a *chavrusah*. With a clear mind, we are able to achieve deep *kavanah* and fire in our tefillah. With a clear mind, we are able to put all our strength into every single mitzvah.

We see the importance of *yishuv hadaas* from the fact that it is the first thing that we ask for in our *Shemoneh Esrei* three times a day. It is the foundation of *all* our physical and spiritual successes.

So, the clear sign to knowing who the tzaddik of our generation depends on: whoever has the ability to help us to do teshuvah through deepening our *yishuv hadaas*. This is the tzaddik who has received the *ruach hakodesh* which was passed down from Moshe Rabbeinu to Yehoshua, and throughout all the generations until today.

When we find such a tzaddik, then we've found our doctor.

It is due to the tzaddik's pure awareness of Hashem that he's able to receive an aspect of *ruach hakodesh*.

It is the tzaddik's own clarity of mind which gives him an aspect of *ruach hakodesh*. Rebbe Nachman explains (Likutei Mohoran I, 54) that Hashem is constantly communicating with us through Divine Providence. This communication manifests itself through the thoughts, speech, and action, which we experience all the time.

However, most of us are completely unaware of Hashem's messages; as our minds are so mixed up with confusion, fears, worries, physical desires, emotions, and imaginations, etc. Our heads are like raw eggs that are constantly being scrambled! We can't focus on anything for more than a second or two; before we get ambushed with foreign thoughts that take over our minds. Therefore, we hardly ever recognize any revelation of Hashem's Divine Providence in our life whatsoever.

On the other hand, the greater a tzaddik is the more he has the ability to overcome all of his bad thoughts and purify his mind. The greater a tzaddik is the more he is able to attain real *yishuv hadaas* and a constant awareness of Hashem. Therefore, a true tzaddik experiences this world in a completely different way than we do. He's able to truly live with Hashem. He's able to attach his thoughts to Him in such a deep way, that he receives an aspect of *ruach hakodesh* – a deep spiritual insight – that no one else can achieve.

This deep spiritual insight is what gives a tzaddik the ability to help us. Since his thoughts are so still and focused, he can quickly see and understand exactly what we're going through. Because of his pure *yishuv hadaas*, his eyes are like X-rays into our mind and soul. He can identify precisely what is the cause of our sickness and give an instant and accurate diagnosis. Then, through his *ruach hakodesh*, he also knows exactly the medicine which we need in order to heal.

Once we know what we're looking for, we must do everything possible to find it.

Using this teaching of Rebbe Nachman; it is possible for even those in the of darkest places to find out precisely whom our tzaddik – our shepherd – truly is. It is possible for us to identify him amongst all the other tzaddikim, simply by following his advice and seeing if it can help us to attach ourselves to Hashem.

Therefore, we have no excuse! We must search for such a tzaddik with every single ounce of strength, we have. We must look in the *sefarim hakadoshim* and see if they're giving us the inspiration that we need. We must try to practice their teachings for a period of time, and see if they can help us. We must go to *shiurim* and meet the tzaddikim of our generation. We must take every opportunity we can to talk to other people who are truly seeking to save their souls from their spiritual illnesses.

Most importantly, we must daven. We must scream to Hashem to assist in finding our doctor. We must cry tearfully to Hashem to help us find our tzaddik and escape our miserable existence. We must plead with Hashem not to let us go to our grave without getting the treatment we need. We must beg Hashem to bring us to the one with all the remedies to bring our heart of stone back to life. When we truly contemplate where we're headed and where we would actually like to be going; then there is no end to the amount of tefillos - we must daven to find our tzaddik.

We must also believe that Hashem is truly compassionate and He very badly wants to help us and all of *klal Yisroel* to do teshuvah and bring Mashiach. Indeed, He hears every single tefillah. He sees every single effort that we make to find His tzaddik, whom He will send to guide us. And when we show Hashem our sincerest desire to find the one who can bring us closer to Him, He will certainly help us.

Even once we've connected to the tzaddik, if we stop searching for his *ruach hakodesh*, we will fall into darkness (see Likutei Halachos, Sheluchim 5).

However, even after we've found the tzaddik who can heal us, we must know that the journey is not over. There is a very common phenomenon which occurs, when we begin to attach ourselves to our true tzaddik. At first, we experience incredible inspiration. We feel good about ourselves and happy with our life. We feel more motivated to serve Hashem than we ever have before. We feel elated, as if we're flying in the clouds. We've never been able to wake up so early and daven with so much *kavanah*. We relish the sweetness of our tefillah. Even though we've never really had a deep connection to learning before; once we find our tzaddik, we can't do anything else. As mentioned above, this is all due to the clarity of mind which the tzaddik helps us to achieve.

But at some point, we sense that we're running out of gas. We watch the gauge of our spiritual inspiration drop slowly – or sometimes even very quickly – until finally we hit the bottom. What happens next is perhaps the most painful thing in the world: From our elevated heights of *deveikus*, we fall to the lowest depths of despair and below...

This is because before we had found our tzaddik, we didn't have any inspiration at all; so things didn't seem so bad. Since most of the people around us were also not so connected to Hashem; we thought that this was normal and everything was okay. We had no idea what we were missing. However, after we've tasted the amazing light of the tzaddik and the sweetness of *yishuv hadaas* in *avodas Hashem*; without it, we feel an extremely deep emptiness. We feel completely broken and burnt out. Without the inspiration of our tzaddik, our tefillah becomes lifeless, and we have to force ourselves to sit down and learn a little bit each day. Sometimes, we don't learn at all. The lights go out and our life becomes completely dark.

Some of us may take this as a sign to completely run away from our tzaddik. We second guess everything that we experienced and we throw it all in the trash. Or perhaps, we may still associate with this tzaddik and follow his teachings, but only in a very superficial way. We may go through the motions of being connected to the tzaddik – davening in his minyan and observing his *minhagim* – but on the inside, we're filled with questions and doubts about him: "What happened to me? Things were going so well and the tzaddik was helping me so much. Now, it feels like he's pushing me so far away from Hashem."

We think that, perhaps, the tzaddik's teachings may be able to help other people who are already stronger in *avodas Hashem*. Or perhaps, they are able to heal us some of the time, but not when we're really messed up. Maybe the tzaddik was able to give us some hope for a little while, and help us make some progress… But in the end, he can't really get us out of the excrement of physical desire that we've been stuck in for decades.

We occasionally reminisce about the "good times" when we felt so inspired. We wait and hope for them to come again. Sometimes, we get a little glimpse, but then our life becomes black again. What's going on?

Rebbe Nachman explains this phenomenon. He says (Likutei Mohoran I, 17:2) that there could be a tzaddik, whose light is great enough to illuminate not only this World but all the Higher Worlds as well. Nevertheless, even someone who is sitting right next to him could be swallowed up by complete darkness. Despite the Eternal Light of Hashem that is shining through the tzaddik; we could be so lost in our own twisted thoughts and actions that we fail to receive that Light at all.

This is because we've stopped searching. We've stopped looking for our tzaddik. What we don't realize is that our initial inspiration was due largely in part to our efforts to find our tzaddik. It was in the merit of our deep desire and our countless tefillos, that we were able to attach ourselves to his teachings and achieve a higher level of *yishuv hadaas*.

However, when we find the tzaddik and stop searching, we lose all of our inspiration. We lose all of our spiritual awakening. Without our constant efforts to attach ourselves further to the tzaddik; he is not able to give us the medicine we need to heal. Thus, we run out of gas and get stuck on the shoulder of the tzaddik's highway.

Reb Nosson explains this in a very simple way; He says that through our initial search we find the tzaddik's physical form – i.e. we come to recognize which tzaddik can help us – but if we stop there and don't continue searching, then we will not find his soul – *ruach hakodesh* – which is the real treatment for our illness. We will fail to acquire the *yishuv hadaas* which brings us to love and awe in our *avodas Hashem*.

We must believe that the tzaddik's teachings are meant specifically for us; no matter far we've fallen.

Therefore, even after we are connected the tzaddik who can heal our sickness; we must continue to look even deeper for his spiritual light. The first thing we must do is daven to Hashem to help us let go of all of our doubts about the tzaddik and have pure faith that he is Hashem's messenger to save us. We must pour out our hearts to the Master of the Universe for help to believe that the path of the tzaddik is specifically for us; even if we've fallen to the lowest depths. We must continue to pray to Hashem for the knowledge that we have the ability to connect to this tzaddik and follow in his ways. We must beg Hashem for help with the belief that if we continue looking; we will rediscover the light of the tzaddik, which we experienced when we first came close to him.

In order to find the tzaddik's light, we must look deeply into his Torah.

Secondly, we must learn the tzaddik's *sefarim* in breadth and depth, and use every bit of strength we have to understand them. If we struggle to grasp a certain teaching, we should look at all of the commentaries available to us. We should daven to Hashem to help us. We should ask Hashem to open our mind to be able to receive the tzaddik's teachings.

If there's any Torah which it is important for us to learn in depth; it is the Torah of our tzaddik. Even though Hashem certainly loves it when we learn the *Gemara be'iyun*; at the end of the day, the most important thing is the actual fulfillment of the mitzvos. Just like our Sages say (Avos, 1:17), "The study [of the Torah] is not the main thing, rather the practice." So, we see from here that it is important for us to learn the clear-cut halachos, in order for us to know exactly what to do.

However, even this is not the most important area of in-depth study, since we could know all the halachos in incredible detail, and still not do any of it. Even though we could have the Torah in our head, our *yetzer harah* could completely stop us from bringing it into action.

Therefore, the most important thing for us to understand indepth is the *sefer* of the tzaddik, since it can give us the advice, inspiration and strength to overcome all of our obstacles and perform Hashem's mitzvos (see Likutei Halachos, Netilas Yadaim 6:91). [Note: This doesn't mean that we should spend all day just learning the *sefer* of the tzaddik. Rather, our primary *limud* should be Gemara and halachah. The point is that more than any other *sefer*, we should try our best to truly understand the *sefer* of the tzaddik in depth, and to know what his advice really is.]

In addition, we should learn the tzaddik's Torah on a daily basis. We must approach it as if it is water and air, which we simply cannot live without. The first thing that we do every day, either before or right after *shacharis*, should be to sit down and open one of his *sefarim*. It should be like our addiction to coffee: we have to get our "fix" at the beginning of each day as soon as humanly (and halachically) possible. Then, whatever we learn that morning from the tzaddik's teachings, we should carry with us the rest of the day. It should be constantly on our mind wherever we go. We should relate to the world and understand everything that happens around us based on his Torah.

We must also learn the Torah of the tzaddik with the intention of bringing his teachings into practice.

However, it is possible to know the *sefer* of a tzaddik backwards and forwards and understand it incredibly in depth, and still be very far away from practicing his teachings. Without bringing the tzaddik's advice into action, we will not be able to receive the his light and *ruach hakodesh*.

Therefore, we must look honestly at ourselves and see if we're actually following the Torah of our tzaddik. "Are we doing what he tells us? Do we at least have a deep desire to follow in his ways?"

If we see that we're lacking, then we must change the way that we approach the study of the tzaddik's Torah. Instead of just trying to understand his teachings, we must learn them with the intention to daven to Hashem to help us fulfill the tzaddik's advice (see Likutei Mohoran II, 25). This means that we shouldn't approach the Torah of the tzaddik as if it is just a good *vort* or a *peshat* in the Gemara. Rather, we must try to grasp the practical advice of his teachings in order to turn them into a tefillah. Then, we should take some time to talk to Hashem and daven to Him to help us fulfill the Torah of the tzaddik that we learned that day.

We should say whatever comes into our heart and beg Hashem for assistance in coming closer to Him, through the advice of the tzaddik. We should express our longing and yearning to truly receive the tzaddik's light so deeply inside our hearts, that it will be able to transform us completely.

The most important aspect of our search for the tzaddik is that we must attach ourselves to his talmidim.

Perhaps, the greatest aspect of a true tzaddik is that he is able to transmit his *ruach hakodesh* to his *talmidim* – like Moshe Rabbeinu to Yehoshua – in such a way, that his light doesn't die away when he passes on to the Next World. He is able to inspire his *talmidim* so deeply that they also burn with a holy fire for Hashem. They receive the spiritual spark of their rebbe so strongly that they're able to guide their generation, and inspire their own *talmidim* as well.

Of course, not every single *talmid* receives the same amount of *ruach hakodesh*. For example, through the strength of Moshe Rabbeinu, all of *klal Yisroel* received *ruach hakodesh* at Har Sinai. We all experienced prophecy when Hashem gave us the first two commandments. However, our level of *ruach hakodesh* could not compare to that of the Levi'im who were the only ones who kept their faith in Moshe Rabbeinu during the sin of the golden calf. And even the Levi'im did not receive the *ruach hakodesh* to the same extent as Yehoshua; who was the only one who could take Moshe Rabbeinu's place, as the leader of the *klal Yisroel*.

How did Yehoshua merit such a lofty position? The verse says (Shemos 33), "And the youth, Yehoshua, did not leave the tent [of Moshe Rabbeinu]." From here, we see that it was only through Yehoshua's persistent search and attachment to his rebbe, that he merited to receive Moshe Rabbeinu's *ruach hakodesh* more than anyone else.

The same is true for the *talmidim* of every tzaddik in every generation. There are many different levels of attachment to a tzaddik; and each *talmid* according to his effort, merits to receive some aspect of the tzaddik's *ruach hakodesh*. However, there can be only one *talmid* who truly receives the light of his rebbe, on the highest level. He is the one who carries the primary torch of inspiration to the next generation.

Therefore, the most important aspect in our search for the *ruach hakodesh* of the tzaddik is to try to find his true *talmidim*; and especially the one who gave up his life to capture the tzaddik's teachings in the deepest way. We simply cannot come close to the tzaddik without his *talmidim*. It is only through them that the spirit of the tzaddik is still alive in this world. They are, so to speak, the stamp of the tzaddik (see Likutei Mohoran I, 140). They are the main connection between us and the tzaddik.

The Torah of the tzadik is like a massive superstore, and his talmidim are the expert salesmen.

To understand the importance of connecting with the primary *talmidim* of the tzaddik, let us take the following parable (based on Chayei Mohoran, 375):

We go to a massive superstore to buy a few things. We step inside the store and we're blinded by all the flashing lights and millions of products before our eyes. We see aisle after aisle with seemingly no end. We are completely lost. We have no idea where to find what we're looking for. We get distracted and start picking up things that we don't really need. We start wandering around aimlessly. If we were left to our own devices, we would end up walking out of the store with a cart full of unnecessary items and we wouldn't find anything on our list.

However, we're not alone. There is a salesman to help us. This salesman knows the entire store inside and out. He's been working there for thirty years already. He arranged the store himself to make it easier for us to find what we need. Not only that, but because of his deep intuition and understanding of his customers' needs, he often knows that what we need is *really* something other than what we *originally* thought. With his help, we end up walking out of the massive superstore, with all the essential things that we were missing in our lives.

So too, the teachings of the tzaddik are so incredibly vast and expansive that it is nearly impossible to find what we really need. Furthermore, most of us don't even know what we're actually missing in our lives. Therefore, without any help, we will certainly fail to get the guidance we're looking for and will leave the tzaddik with a feeling of deep despair.

However, the tzaddik would never leave his superstore of Torah without a salesman. In every generation, there has to be a *talmid* of the tzaddik who understands and practices the teachings of the tzaddik on a very deep level. There has to be a *talmid* who has searched so hard for the light of the tzaddik, that he's able to arrange all of the tzaddik's teachings and put them in their proper place. Not only that; but he also has received the aspect of *ruach hakodesh* that allows him the insight to comprehend exactly what our needs are and be able to guide us to the right aisle.

So too, we must search for such a *talmid* just like we searched for the tzaddik. We must do all the same things mentioned above, in order to find him. With this, we will come to recognize this *talmid* through using the same sign with which we identified the tzaddik himself: We will receive a greater awareness of Hashem. That same *ruach hakodesh* which we tasted when we first came close to the tzaddik himself; we will receive in abundance when we connect ourselves to his primary *talmid*.

Nevertheless, even once we've found the true *talmid* our journey is not over. We must constantly search and yearn for more. We must constantly look to find an even deeper level of *ruach hakodesh* from the tzaddik, through the channels mentioned above. It is our *ratzon* and effort that brings us closer to the tzaddik and allows us to receive continuous inspiration.

With this *ratzon*, we will see that we're never alone in our struggles. We will see that Hashem has sent us a messenger to heal us. Through our search, the tzaddik will be able to transform our entire being. He will help us achieve our greatest potential in *avodas Hashem*, and pave the way for us to reach a lofty destination in the Next World, amen!